Last Years
of the
WAVERLEY ROUTE

Last Years
of the
WAVERLEY ROUTE

David Cross

An imprint of
Ian Allan Publishing

Front cover: **Making good progress near Fountainhall on the morning of 2 September 1965 is Class B1 4-6-0 No 61354. The 'B1' at this stage was only 16 years old, having been built at Darlington in 1949. The train is the 6.58am Hawick–Edinburgh, a journey taking 88 minutes for the 53 miles. By this time these duties were shared with the BRCW/Sulzer Type 2 (later Class 26) diesels.** John Spencer Gilks

Back cover: **'Royal Scot' 4-6-0 No 46115** *Scots Guardsman* **leaves Galashiels on 18 July 1965 with an Edinburgh Waverley–Carlisle stopper. The locomotive was withdrawn in December 1965, and some claim that this was the last time** *Scots Guardsman* **worked a passenger service for British Rail. After decades out of sight, one of the highlights of 2008 was its return to the main line.** Richard Barbour / Colour-Rail

Half-title: **Night photographs were not so common in the 1960s. This one is full of atmosphere. Class 7P6F Pacific No 70003** *John Bunyan* **stands at Carlisle Citadel with driver Willie Box on the footplate, ready to depart with a train of ECS. Towards the end of steam (No 70003 was withdrawn in March 1967), steam locomotives were not maintained very well and were certainly not cleaned. Often, as here, only the number was given a wipe. Driver Box has a handful of cotton waste, which was often used for that purpose.** Peter Brock

Right: **No book featuring Edinburgh would be complete without a picture of Edinburgh Castle taken from Princes Street Gardens. The train photographed just west of Waverley station is a Glasgow Queen Street to London King's Cross through service seen here hauled by BRCW Type 2 No D5365. This locomotive would give-way to a Type 4 in Waverley station for the onward journey. Later Class 27 No 27019, it was in service for 23 years and always allocated to sheds in Scotland. This picture was taken on 26 May 1965.** Derek Cross

First published 2010

ISBN 978 0 86093 633 6

© David Cross 2010

Published by Oxford Publishing Co

An imprint of Ian Allan Publishing Ltd, Hersham, Surrey, KT12 4RG.
Printed in England by Ian Allan Printing Ltd, Hersham, Surrey, KT12 4RG.

Distributed in Canada and the United States of America by BookMasters Distribution Services.

Visit the Ian Allan Publishing website at www.ianallanpublishing.com

The Waverley route closed early in 1969, more than 40 years ago, when I was in my early teens. It was less than 100 miles long and served very limited population centres along its route. My own recollections of the line are not very extensive. I remember travelling over the line once on a school trip from Edinburgh to Carlisle behind a Class 45 diesel, but as the West Bromwich Albion football team was also on the train, we spent most of the journey trying to get the players' autographs. I also made a number of photographic trips to the line with my father, Derek Cross, who, I think, found it difficult to get as far as the Waverley route from our then home in Ayrshire. The journey from Ayr to Hawick was not an easy one, and for Derek it was made more difficult by the need to cross the Nith Valley line and the Clyde Valley line, and the many interesting branches in between, on the way to the Waverley route. On more than one occasion, I remember, we set off for the Waverley route but did not get there because we had found something unexpected and interesting on the way. For example, passing New Cumnock very early one morning at the beginning of the 1960s, we noticed Standard Class 2 2-6-0 No 77018, which was taking over from a failed 'Coronation' Pacific, No 46249 *City of Sheffield*, on the northbound Euston–Glasgow sleeping-car train. This unusual working delayed us so long that we never reached the Waverley route on what was to have been my first visit. At other times, events on Beattock prevented us from getting to Hawick, and I recall that the weather thwarted our efforts on several occasions; but the times when my father did get there were rewarding, and he took some fine pictures on the line.

Steam traction over the Waverley route continued into December 1966, when Dundee-based Class B1 4-6-0 No 61278 headed a Carlisle–Edinburgh train. Derek had taken pictures of this beautifully turned-out locomotive at Kilmarnock on its way south to Carlisle, and he had every intention of going across to the Waverley route to record the special heading north through the desolate hills around Newcastleton and Whitrope Summit, which in early December would be at their wildest best; at least, that had been the plan until his Rover 2000 broke down on the way. This caused great frustration, as might be imagined, and prompted a rant about how the Sunbeam Alpine that the Rover had replaced would have got him there for sure. Much worse was to follow, when the Rover broke down again 18 months later, on 11 August 1968 — the last day of main-line steam in Britain! The errant car was abandoned at Appleby and, for all my father cared, could have remained there for ever!

The Waverley route is still remembered with affection some 40 years after its closure. This book tries to recapture some typical scenes and events, and some of the trains and people that were active in its final years.

David Cross
Brentwood
June 2010

ACKNOWLEDGEMENTS

Obtaining new material of any quality on a line that closed over forty years ago has been very challenging. Apart from the material of my late father, Derek Cross, I have had to ask for support and help from many others. The volume of assistance has been very welcome, very sincere and somewhat unexpected, with everyone keen to see the results of these efforts in this book. I think that this is simply because the book is about a railway that still attracts great interest.

First, I should like to thank all the photographers who have been very helpful and allowed me to use both their colour and their black-and-white material. Peter Brock died in April 2007; his widow, Sylvia, has been very generous in allowing me access to his photographs. His are the train crew and footplate pictures, and those of Carlisle Canal shed. Derek Cross took very few photographs of locomotive sheds, so Peter's filled a gap in my father's otherwise extensive collection.

Ron White's Colour-Rail has, as ever, helped enormously with some of the colour material; I should like to wish Ron a long and happy retirement.

I should also like to mention Gavin Morrison, Brian Stephenson, Neville Stead, John Beckett, John Spencer Gilks and Mike Esau for their invaluable help. I do hope you enjoy their efforts on these pages as well.

In a wider context I would mention Winston Cole, who told me what a good idea a book on the Waverley route would be, and how such a book would help the nascent Waverley Route Heritage Association with their efforts at Whitrope.

My armchair Waverley route expert, friend and critic in Liverpool, Norman Russell, has been on at me for years to further explore the Waverley route, a line that he is still determined to 'do' again, this time as a 98-mile walk!

I should also like to mention the stranger who last year helped me to navigate the one-way ring road system in Galashiels, ending up in the Asda car park! I had gone back to Galashiels to see what remained of the Waverley route, and stopped to ask a middle-aged man where the old station was. He looked at me blankly and told me, in that wonderful Borders accent, that there was no railway station in Galashiels. This disconnect lasted about thirty seconds, until I asked him how old he was. He said he was thirty-eight, so he was much too young to remember the station! He did however accept a lift. On the short journey I recognised some of the old railway formation, and followed it to Asda. Where the old Galashiels station used to be there is now a health centre, where, on the waiting-room wall, four large, high-quality black-and-white prints commemorate the former use of the site.

Especially, I should like to thank my wife, Jane, for helping with the word processing, grammar and compilation of the captions; her work has been a real help. Secondly, I thank my mother, Elizabeth, for allowing my father to get away to the lineside to record the railway as it was in the beautiful Borders half a century ago.

I have had to include one or two pictures that have been published before, although most of them some years ago, for which nevertheless I offer an apology in advance. To illustrate this point, the quality point, I have a picture of Class A4 Pacific No 60026 *Miles Beevor* inside the shed at Galashiels on 11 January 1964, but its quality is so poor that it simply cannot be published.

Once more I'd like to thank all the contributors who have helped me, and I also hope that all readers enjoy this book about a fabulous railway line.

INTRODUCTION

The period covered by this book is broadly the last 15 years of the Waverley route, roughly from 1954 to 1969. During this time, throughout the country, steam was giving way to diesel, and the system was having to cope with the impact of Dr Richard Beeching's famous cuts. Many aspects of the railway network changed dramatically and for ever, but in those years long ago, even the name British Rail had yet to be invented.

I have arranged this book in a geographical progression from north to south, covering Edinburgh, Hawick and Carlisle and the sections in between. Edinburgh and Carlisle are, of course, substantial centres of railway interest in their own right. I have also added a section about the footplate men who worked hard to ensure that

their steam locomotives performed so well in some pretty inhospitable places. This applied both on the footplate, especially in the tunnels, and off the footplate, on the wilder country sections of the Waverley route.

My aim has been to illustrate as much variety of motive power and location as possible. I have also tried to maximise the number of classes depicted, from Caledonian Railway Single No 123, built in 1886, to an 'EE' Type 3 diesel of 1964. There are also a couple of pictures of industrial tank engines operated by the National Coal Board in the Lothians coalfield. Likewise the great variety of traffic is featured, from the named 'Waverley' express to London to a diesel shunter, hauling a pick-up freight, wandering off to Greenlaw on the branch east of St Boswells.

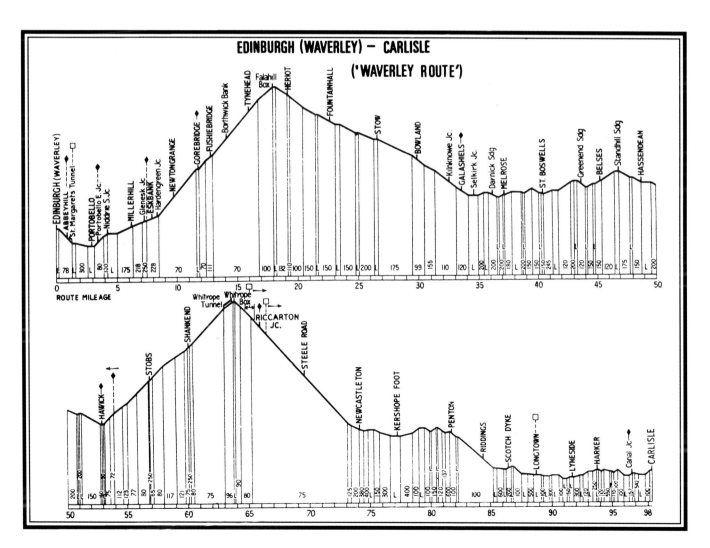

Above: **A classic 1950s Waverley-route freight sees 'K3' No 60895 plod towards Riccarton Junction with a northbound freight from Carlisle to Niddrie yard during September 1958.** Peter Brock

The route described

The Waverley route was built by the North British Railway Company, and was opened in two stages, from Edinburgh to Hawick in 1849 and thence to Carlisle by 1862. The name appears to have been inspired by Sir Walter Scott's 'Waverley' novels, as many of the stories were set in the surrounding countryside.

The entire route had an 'edge', an atmosphere of men and machines battling against the elements. It was almost as if every summit that was climbed successfully was an achievement. The route that the railway followed through the Border hills could be fearsome. Wind, rain, mist and snow were often in evidence, sometimes all in a single day. The endless curvature of the line and the wild country, with more sheep than people, added to the recipe for the battle between the railway and the stark moorland country that prevailed, particularly on the southern section. There was little habitation apart from the main towns of Hawick, Melrose, St Boswells and Galashiels. However, there were some most interesting places, even if they were not large centres of population.

Riccarton Junction had a claim to be the most remarkable. It was literally in the middle of nowhere, 32 miles from Carlisle and 66 from Edinburgh. There was no road access. The station was opened in October 1862, and

a railway village grew up around the site. The reason for its existence was its presence at the point where the Border Counties line from Hexham met the Waverley route. Eventually, the buildings at Riccarton included an engine shed for six locomotives, an engineering shop, the station itself and two signalboxes. At its height, the population of Riccarton probably reached about 120. The only access was by rail, largely to and from Hawick, 12 miles away. Reportedly it was the Co-op in Hawick that supplied the inhabitants of Riccarton with food. This was, of course, carried by train every day, and it was those same trains that would take the children at Riccarton to and from school in Hawick. Emergency doctors, if needed, also had to get to Riccarton by train from Hawick through the wild hills around Whitrope and past the forbidding Arnton Fell.

After the closure of the Border Counties line at the end of 1956, and, 13 years later, that of the Waverley route itself, the population gradually declined, and of the more than thirty houses that made up the original settlement only one remains occupied today.

Changing traction

During its final years the Waverley route enjoyed a rich variety of steam and diesel traction. At the southern end of the line, Carlisle Canal shed closed in June 1963, making Carlisle essentially an ex-LMS stronghold. Meanwhile, at the other end of the line in Edinburgh, most of the motive power was provided by ex-LNER locomotives. Thus the Waverley route had access to both sets of locomotives, and to them were added the diesels, which began to appear during the late 1950s. Noted on the route were Clayton Type 1s (later TOPS Class 17), Sulzer-engined Type 2s built either by BR itself (Classes 24 and 25) or by BRCW (Class 26), English Electric Type 3s (Class 37) and Type 4s (Class 40), BR and Brush Type 4s (Classes 45, 46 and 47) and English Electric 'Deltic' Type 5s (Class 55), all of which are featured in these pages.

The end of steam

At the end of steam on the Waverley route, BR, LMS and LNER types were still at work. The last steam-hauled stopping train from Hawick to Carlisle left on 5 June 1965, and was worked by BR Standard Class 4 2-6-0 No 76050. That same year the last three active Class A3 Pacifics – Nos 60041 *Salmon Trout*, 60052 *Prince Palatine* and (a favourite of Derek Cross) 60100 *Spearmint* – were still at work.

As mentioned elsewhere in the book, the drastic culling of the 'V2s' meant that only thirteen were left in traffic in 1965. Of these, five were based at Dundee, and eight at Edinburgh St Margarets, so it was on the Waverley route that this most successful class of 2-6-2s in service remained in service until their final demise in mid-1966.

Towards the end, when special trains started running, the variety of motive power increased. Visiting locomotives, both steam and diesel, began to appear. As late as September 1966 steam 'farewell' trains were run over the line, using Class V2 No 60836 which was a Dundee Tay Bridge locomotive. Just a month later, another Dundee-based locomotive, Class A2 4-6-2 No 60532 *Blue Peter*, worked the 'A2' farewell tour on 8 October 1966. A month after that, Class A4 4-6-2 No 60019 *Bittern* turned out to work an Edinburgh–Leeds railtour. Happily, both *Blue Peter* and *Bittern* are now preserved.

Final motive power

Even after steam had gone, the variety continued up to the closure of the line. By that time, the expresses were being worked by Class 45 and Class 46 'Peak' diesels, and Class 55 'Deltics' and Class 47s appeared on the 'farewell specials'. The local services were mainly in the hands of Class 26s, with Classes 25 and 37 putting in an appearance from time to time.

Freight traffic also saw great variety; Clayton Class 17 No D8578, Class 25 No D7607, Class 26 No D5308 and Class 40 No D368 were all seen on freight workings in the early months of 1969. Freight traffic ceased on 25 April 1969, soon after the closure to passengers on 5 January that year. Then the whole line closed and demolition began.

What remains?

Parts of the old line remain in use as part of the modern rail network. The Waverley route left the East Coast main line at Portobello Junction and passed through Niddrie and, further on, the Millerhill marshalling yard, before reaching the first station at Eskbank, 8 miles from Edinburgh Waverley. Over the last 25 years, Edinburgh has expanded, and Niddrie, 4 miles from Waverley and then on the outskirts, is now very much part of the city. Close to Niddrie there had been a coal mine, Newcraighall Colliery, which went out under the Firth of Forth. It closed at about the same time as the Waverley route, but the section of the railway from Portobello Junction to Millerhill remained open, to give access to the yard and to the circular Edinburgh suburban lines, now freight-only.

Today, these two lines run as parallel single lines for some distance, though they appear to be a double-track railway. Since 2002, this section of the old line has become both busier and more relevant, as from June of that year passenger traffic was resumed. As Edinburgh has grown, it has become more congested, and the need for a rail service from the east has increased. New stations at Brunstane and Newcraighall opened on 3 June 2002. Brunstane was built with a simple single platform, but Newcraighall is a much larger interchange station, with a bus interchange and a very large car park for 'park and ride' users.

Another reason for the station at Newcraighall was the construction of a very large retail park at nearby Fort Kinnaird. It and Brunstane were reportedly the first new stations on a reopened main line since rail privatisation in the mid-1990s. The trains were half-hourly, and ran across the city via Waverley and Haymarket to Dunblane or Bathgate. Later they ran to Kirkcaldy and Cowdenbeath in Fife, but the 'cross-city' concept remains intact. By all accounts these 'new' passenger services on the 'old' Waverley route formation have been a real success; they will, one hopes, lead to the reopening of another section of the Waverley route beyond Newcraighall.

At the Carlisle end, the stub of the Waverley route remains in use, giving access to the Carlisle Storage freight yard at Brunthill. The famous bridge at Kingmoor, which took the Waverley route over the West Coast main line, still sees occasional traffic.

Future aspirations

And so what of the future? Throughout the forty years since the Waverley route closed, various schemes to rebuild and reopen parts of the line have been mooted.

As steam finished in 1968, there was a plan to save the whole line from Edinburgh to Carlisle for running steam locomotives after British Rail had banned their use. It came to nothing, as did the reinstatement of a single line from Carlisle to near Newcastleton, to help the movement of timber from the extensive forestry developments in and around Kielder Forest.

Of all the schemes, one of the most recent now appears the most likely to succeed: the reopening of the northern end of the Waverley route by the Scottish Parliament as a commuter railway. In recent years the Parliament and the Scottish Executive have made real efforts to maximise the use of rail transport and the rail infrastructure, much of which remains, some of it albeit derelict. This initiative entails not only the reopening of closed stations but also the reopening and electrification of an entire closed railway, the line from Glasgow through Airdrie and Bathgate to Edinburgh.

Above: **This photograph, taken from the upper reaches of Carlisle Canal depot, possibly from the coaling stage, puts the location in the context of the Waverley route, the River Eden and the northern suburbs of the city of Carlisle. Class J36 0-6-0 No 65321 is in the foreground, already in store in the shed yard before its scrapping at the end of 1962. Passing on the viaduct over the River Eden is the up 'Waverley', slowing for the Carlisle stop, behind an unidentified 'Peak' diesel. Beyond the third coach of the 'Waverley' is the bridge that carries the West Coast main line over the River Eden, and immediately to the left of that is the suburb of Kingmoor. This was home to the famous 12A steam shed, now a nature reserve. On the other side of the West Coast main line is the present diesel depot, maintaining a locomotive depot link with that part of Carlisle that goes back over 100 years.**
Peter Brock

There are now firm plans to reopen a commuter railway from Edinburgh Waverley to a new station at Tweedbank, a short distance from Galashiels. It would use the formation of the Waverley route from Millerhill to Galashiels, a distance of about 35 miles. The aim is to boost the local economy along the route, to assist commuting to Edinburgh and to ease traffic congestion in the city. Royal Assent was given to the enabling legislation in 2006, and it is estimated that more than 200,000 people could benefit from the re-establishment of the railway. Although subsequently delayed, there is now real hope that the revamped Waverley route will proceed.

This plan was reaffirmed by the Scottish Transport Minister, Stewart Stevenson, towards the end of 2009. In outline, it looks as though the railway will offer a half-hourly diesel-unit service from Edinburgh Waverley to Tweedbank, calling at a new station at Shawfair (on the site of the former Monktonhall colliery), then Eskbank, Newtongrange, Gorebridge, Stow, Galashiels, all reopened original Waverley-route stations and another new station at Tweedbank.

The journey would take just 55 minutes each way for the 36-mile journey. The cost of rebuilding this part of the Waverley route is estimated to be around £295 million. Apart from the environmental benefits, road accidents would be reduced on the A7 and A68 trunk roads and 450,000 tonnes of carbon would be saved over 60 years.

The reopening would help to regenerate the area served by the entire northern section of the line, as well as easing the traffic congestion on the roads to and from Edinburgh. How sensible a basic railway in the area would be! From the single-carriageway A7, especially between Gorebridge and Stow, where the old formation runs

close by, one can still catch a glimpse of a bridge or the old trackbed from the twisty road. The formation is still in place, waiting to be refurbished, with track relaid and reopened, for the benefit of local people, local communities and railway enthusiasts.

By 2014 it should be possible to return to Falahill and photograph a passenger train more than 45 years after Derek Cross stood there, doing just that.

It bodes well for the project that all the property required to build the line has been acquired, ground and structural surveys have been completed and some pipes and cables moved near Galashiels in early 2010. The 'Border Railway Project', it seems, is under way, and the railway line to Tweedbank will open during 2014. Railway enthusiasts would love to see an Class A1 4-6-2 with just one different digit in the number — No 60163 *Tornado* as opposed to No 60162 *St Johnstoun* — once more racing through Tynehead and on to Galashiels. Here's hoping!

Below: **A picture taken in June 2009 and featuring a passenger train on the formation of the old Waverley route. Class 67 diesel No 67 025 *Western Star* passes Brunstane station with empty coaching stock from Millerhill Yard to Edinburgh Waverley, where it will form a 'Fife Circle' passenger service. Coincidentally, 'Britannia' Pacific No 70025, also named *Western Star*, was allocated to Carlisle Kingmoor shed in 1966/7, and would, in all probability, also have passed this spot, then better known as Niddrie Junction.** Author

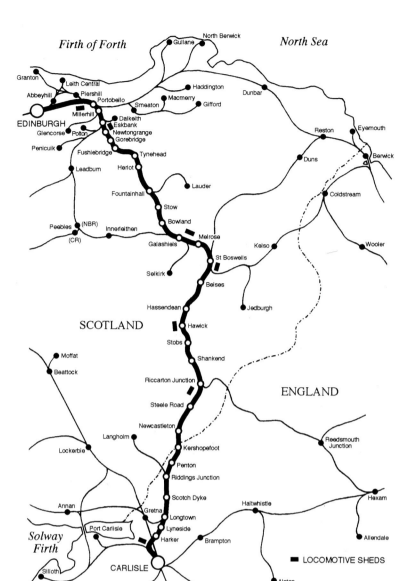

Firth of Forth

North Sea

Left: **The Waverley route with branches and other lines.**

Below: **Sample timetable.**

SCOTLAND

ENGLAND

Solway Firth

CARLISLE

■ LOCOMOTIVE SHEDS

W32											W33

EDINBURGH TO CARLISLE

UP TRAINS — WEEKDAYS

For Timing Notes, see page 35.

Right: **The Waverley station pilot, Class J83 0-6-0T No 68481, is seen here shunting stock through the Mound Tunnel early in October 1950. The 'J83s' were 'specialist' station pilots to be found at Waverley and at Glasgow Queen Street, where the sound of their Westinghouse steam brake and their exhaust bark made them easily identifiable. No 68481, the last numerically of the class of 40, was a minor celebrity. In 1947 the LNER gave it a light-green livery, which lasted into BR days, as seen here. This locomotive was built for the North British Railway in 1901 and remained in service until February 1962.** Derek Cross

Below: **Ex-LNER Class B1 4-6-0 No 61029** *Chamois* **creeps through the suburban platform at Edinburgh Waverley on 16 April 1966 with the empty coaching stock from a football special. Built in 1947 and (in common with all but one of the first batch of forty 'B1s' turned out by Darlington) named after a species of antelope, No 61029 was withdrawn later in 1966, after a working life of just 19 years.** Derek Cross

Left: **Photographed in May 1966, BR Standard Class 4 2-6-4T No 80114 (built at Doncaster in December 1954) brings some empty stock from Craigentinny into Edinburgh Waverley. Just discernible on the cab side is the tablet-catching apparatus, used on single-line sections and common on Scottish-based locomotives. With its 64A shed plate clearly visible, No 809114 is an Edinburgh St Margarets locomotive.** Derek Cross

Below: **For its first 3 miles, as far as Portobello Junction, the Waverley route shared the metals of the East Coast main line. Here Class A4 Pacific No 60024 *Kingfisher* sets off from Waverley with an A4 Preservation Society special to York on a murky day in May 1966. By this time it had been allocated to Aberdeen Ferryhill, along with the other four surviving 'A4s'. One of the last two to remain in traffic (the other was No 60019 *Bittern*), it would eventually be withdrawn in September 1966, after a career of nearly 30 years.** Derek Cross

Above: **Gresley Class A3 Pacific No 4472 *Flying Scotsman* at Edinburgh Waverley in May 1968. It is on a special to King's Cross, and has the double tender used to increase water capacity. Passing by is one of the Swindon-built DMUs that for so long worked the Edinburgh Waverley–Glasgow Queen Street service that was replaced in 1971 by a locomotive-hauled service.** Derek Cross

Below: **A classic view of Edinburgh Waverley in May 1968. This is the east end of the station, watched over by the bridges and the North British Hotel. The train is an ECS movement from the station to Craigentinny carriage sidings. The locomotive, BR/Sulzer Type 2 No D5070, had been allocated from new in 1960 to March depot in East Anglia, and, as No 24 070, was withdrawn from Edinburgh's Haymarket shed in February 1976.** Derek Cross

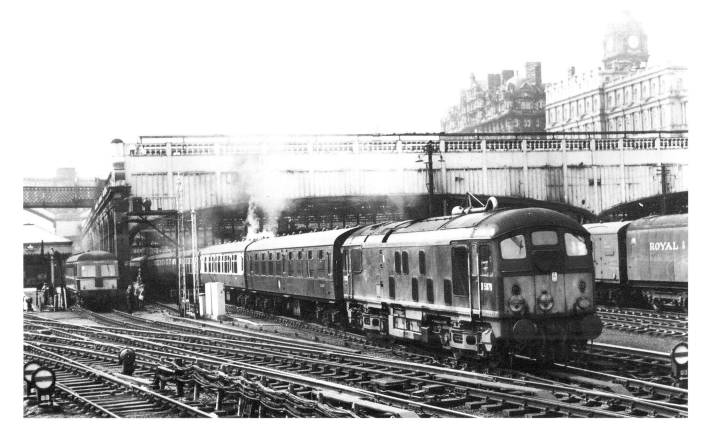

Above: **The present Musselburgh station is on the East Coast main line. The original station was at the other end of the town about a mile away, and formed the terminus of a short branch from Newhailes Junction. In this photograph the last passenger train — a Branch Line Society special returning to Edinburgh — is seen leaving the old station on 27 August 1966, drawn across the River Esk by Class J36 0-6-0 No 65345. Built by the North British Railway at Cowlairs in December 1900, the locomotive was not withdrawn until June 1967, after 67 years' service.** Derek Cross

Below: **The 'full set' of LNER Pacific power on shed at St Margarets, Edinburgh, in 1965. From left to right are 'A4' No 60034 *Lord Faringdon*, 'A3' No 60052 *Prince Palatine*, 'A2' No 60530 *Sayajirao* and 'A1' No 60121 *Silurian* (by now without its nameplates), all in steam and awaiting their next turn of duty.** Neville Stead

Above: **This is Portobello Junction, with the Waverley route coming in from the top right to join the East Coast main line for the last 3 miles into Edinburgh Waverley. The train is an East Coast main-line express, the 12.00pm London King's Cross–Edinburgh Waverley, behind Class 55 'Deltic' No 9001 *St Paddy*. It is the evening of 6 June 1971, the express from London having taken around six hours. The present-day service takes just four and a half hours. The line is now, of course, completely electrified.** Author

Below: **Haymarket-allocated Class D30 4-4-0 No 62437 *Adam Woodcock* on a southbound freight at Portobello on 9 August 1956, heading for the Waverley route with a rake of aged private-owner wagons, destined probably for Hawick.** Gavin Morrison

Above: **Complete with headboard, Class A4 Pacific No 60033 *Seagull* sets off from Portobello Junction for King's Cross with the up 'Elizabethan' on 29 August 1956. The train is using the Waverley route because floods that summer had caused the ECML in Berwickshire to be closed for some weeks, necessitating such Waverley-route diversions. The route was not known for its named trains, the 'Thames–Forth' (later the 'Waverley') being about the only one.** Gavin Morrison

Below: **Class A2 Pacific No 60535 *Hornets Beauty*, a regular Waverley-route performer, passes Portobello Junction, 3 miles from journey's end at Edinburgh Waverley. The train is a Waverley-route semi-fast from Carlisle; its journey will have taken a little over three hours. In August 1958 Portobello still appears to be semi-rural. Now much more built-up, this section of the former Waverley route still sees local passenger services to and from Newcraighall. Towards the end of its working life in 1964/5, *Hornets Beauty* was one of a number of 'A2s' that were cascaded to the former Glasgow & South Western and Caledonian Railway lines.** Derek Cross

18

Above: **Portobello Junction in summer 1964. An Edinburgh Waverley–King's Cross express is headed by the almost new Brush Type 4 No D1545, later No 47 431, built in October 1963. This picture is characterised by a number of empty freight yards, the bulk of the Edinburgh wagonload traffic having been transferred by this time to the new Millerhill marshalling yard.** Derek Cross

Below: **The south end of Millerhill Yard, where the Waverley route left on its way south. In September 1971 a northbound train of oil tanks arrives, emphasising the size of the yard. The locomotive is a very clean, perhaps ex-works, 'Peak', No D187; built in 1962, it later became No 46 050, and worked until 1982. Also of interest is the MGR coal train on the left, with its air-braked brake van. These were used to facilitate propelling moves to coalfields in the Lothians. Although the Waverley route had closed in 1969, the large freight yards at Carlisle Kingmoor and Edinburgh Millerhill continued to see substantial use. Both remain in use today, albeit with much-reduced activity. Author**

Top: **A local Millerhill trip working sets off from the south end of the yard on 7 September 1971. The train is hauled by a 1160hp BR/Sulzer Type 2 diesel, No 5071 (later 24 071), which was withdrawn from nearby Haymarket depot in summer 1975. In the distance, beyond the locomotive, are many of the Swindon-built DMUs that had been displaced from the Glasgow Queen Street–Edinburgh Waverley service in 1971 by the 'new' high-speed service with a Class 27 diesel at each end of six Mk 2 coaches. The site of Millerhill Yard and its relatively low usage from the moment it was constructed made it ideal for the storage of wagons, diesel units and locomotives; the Class 17 'Clayton' diesels above proving this point.** Author

Above: **The Clayton Type 1s were not a great success, the first (No D8500) being put into traffic in September 1962 and the last withdrawn as early as December 1971. Once withdrawn, those in Scotland were moved to either the west coast at Ardrossan or to the east coast at Millerhill Yard. Millerhill is seen here on 11 March 1972, No D8586 leading 14 others of the class. One of them, No D8568, later saw a spell in industrial use and is now preserved in Oxfordshire.** Derek Cross

Right: **Class 25 and Class 26 diesels at Millerhill depot one Sunday morning in April 1977, before being put to work on (mainly) coal-related workings the next day. These two classes and the Class 20s provided freight haulage in and around Edinburgh during much of the 1970s and 1980s. No 25 014 remained in traffic for just three months longer before being scrapped at Glasgow Works. No 26 005 soldiered on but did not join any of her 13 sisters in preservation. There was always plenty of power on shed here, especially at weekends.** Author

Below: **In this May 1964 photograph, a southbound mixed freight is seen between Millerhill Yard and Monktonhall Junction. It is probably heading for Tyne Yard, just south of Newcastle. The train is headed by Pacific Class A1 No 60150 *Willbrook*, one of a number of former express passenger steam locomotives that had been relegated to fitted freights such as this after the advent of the 'Deltics' and various Type 4 diesels in the early 1960s.** Derek Cross

21

Above: **Seen here in August 1958, Millerhill Yard had yet to be enlarged. This long coal train, a mixture of wooden-bodied and more modern steel coal wagons, heads into the yard from the south, perhaps from Lady Victoria Colliery, near Newtongrange, 4 miles back along the Waverley route. The train is hauled, tender-first, by 'J37' 0-6-0 No 64607. Designed and built by Reid for the North British Railway in 1919, the locomotive was withdrawn and scrapped at the end of 1962.** Derek Cross

Below: **Millerhill in August 1958; facing towards Edinburgh. The site of the new Millerhill Yard appears to have been fenced off, but there is little evidence of construction. Elsewhere the site can be seen as it had become by 1963; here, the scene looks like a lunar landscape. A train from Edinburgh to Carlisle via Hawick is hauled by local Class B1 4-6-0 No 61388, then a mere seven years old, having been built by North British in Glasgow in 1951.** Derek Cross

Above: **The new Millerhill marshalling yard, seen here taking shape in August 1958. A down fitted freight from Carlisle arrives behind Class B1 4-6-0 No 61007 *Klipspringer*, which had been built at Darlington in April 1944. The first 'B1' locomotives began building in December 1942, but because of the war it took over 10 years to complete the whole class of 410 locomotives. No 61007 remained in traffic until February 1964.** Derek Cross

Right: **Millerhill also had a locomotive servicing facility. Pictured together on 7 May 1964 are Clayton Type 1 diesel No D8534 and Gresley Class A3 Pacific No 60092 *Fairway*, of Gateshead shed (52A). For many years St Margarets shed was 64A; after it closed, Millerhill adopted that code in April 1967. The changeover years often saw steam and diesel locomotives on the same depot for fuel and basic maintenance. It must have been a nightmare to manage, such were the different demands of the respective traction types, as is confirmed by the modern yard control tower and the aged water tank on the left.** Derek Cross

Above left: **On a hazy morning at the end of August 1958 at Monktonhall Junction, an Edinburgh Waverley–Newcastle train heads south behind Class A2 Pacific No 60518 *Tehran*. The stock, including a bogie luggage van immediately behind the locomotive, has a distinct LNER look to it. *Tehran* was built at Doncaster in December 1946 and remained in traffic only until October 1962. Another Class A2, No 60532 *Blue Peter*, is both the only 'A2' preserved and also the last LNER-designed Pacific to remain in service, being withdrawn in December 1966.**
Derek Cross

Left: **A coal train from one of the pits around Smeaton passes Monktonhall Junction heading for Millerhill Yard in June 1958. The East Coast main line runs parallel to the freight train. The locomotive is Gresley Class J38 No 65929, built in 1926 and bearing a '6F' power classification. The 'J38s' spent their entire working lives in Scotland, mainly engaged on heavy coal trains.**
Derek Cross

Top: **As steam gave way to diesel in this area from about 1960 onwards, Pacifics began to be used in ways that would have been unknown in the 1950s. Here, on 7 July 1962, Class A3 Pacific No 60099 *Call Boy* is pictured at Monktonhall Junction on what appears to be a plain, simple coal train. It was withdrawn in October 1963 and stored at Bathgate shed before being sold to the Scottish scrap dealer, Arnott Young of Carmyle. Fifteen of the 'A3s' met their end in Scotland and the rest in England, the majority at Doncaster or Darlington Works.** Derek Cross

Above: **This is a Branch Line Society special seen in October 1965 on the Roslin branch, near Gilmerton, in the area around Millerhill. It is hauled by preserved GNSR 4-4-0 No 49 *Gordon Highlander*. The combined effect of a large capital city and nearby coalfields caused many branch lines to be built around Edinburgh, many of them serving very small communities. The spoil heap on the right is evidence of local mining activities.**
Derek Cross

Above: **Class A3 Pacific No 60042 *Singapore* approaches Eskbank station, 8 miles from Edinburgh, on 9 May 1964. Having started from Millerhill Yard, a couple of miles away, the southbound freight for Carlisle is now well into the journey and the climb to Falahill. Although it is 1 in 228 through Eskbank, the gradient stiffens to 1 in 70 just after the station at Hardengreen Junction. After its transfer from Newcastle Heaton to Edinburgh St Margarets, *Singapore* became a regular performer on the Waverley route.** Derek Cross

Below: **In January 1969 an Andrew Barclay 0-4-2ST (works number 1193) of 1910, by now carrying the NCB identity Lothian Area No. 6, is busy with a rake of BR 16-ton coal wagons at Lady Victoria Colliery, a deep mine just 10 miles from the centre of Edinburgh. The occasion gave Derek additional reason to journey to the northern end of the Waverley route, which ran alongside the transfer sidings near the village of Newtongrange. He had had great fun in the Ayrshire coalfield with the NCB 'Pugs', which were also Andrew Barclay locomotives built at Kilmarnock, and another Andrew Barclay locomotive did not seem out of place on the opposite side of the country at Lady Victoria.** Derek Cross

Right: **Lothian Area No 6 at Lady Victoria Colliery with some BR wagons. The photograph was taken on a rare sunny winter day, 28 January 1969. The site is now occupied by the Scottish Mining Museum, and is reportedly the finest surviving Victorian colliery in Europe. It is certainly a most interesting site, with the winding engine still *in situ*, a pithead tour available and a selection of mining machinery. When the colliery was visited in early 2009, an Andrew Barclay 0-4-0ST was found hidden away under cover, this one West Ayr Area No 21 (2284/49), being a former NCB Waterside locomotive.** Derek Cross

Below: **Clayton Type 1 (Class 17) No D8530 sets off from the well-filled British Rail / National Coal Board (NCB) transfer sidings at Lady Victoria Colliery on 3 July 1965, bound for Millerhill Yard just 4 miles away. The double track on the right is the Waverley route south towards the next station at Gorebridge. No D8530 was built in 1963; after a very short working life, some of which was spent in store, the end came at Glasgow Works in October 1971.** Derek Cross

Above: **On a long fitted freight from Millerhill Yard, Stanier Class 5 4-6-0 No 45254 is seen here on 30 July 1965, heading south and well into the 12-mile climb to Falahill Summit. The ruling gradient at this point, as the line passes the signalbox opposite Lady Victoria Colliery, is a steady 1 in 70. The 'Black Five' was allocated to Carlisle Kingmoor shed, as attested by the name painted on the buffer-beam and the '12A' shed plate. This one was built by Armstrong Whitworth in 1936. It lasted right up to the end of BR steam in 1968.** Derek Cross

Left: **English Electric 1-Co-Co-1 Type 4 No D214 *Antonia*, with a southbound freight, passes Lady Victoria Colliery on the climb to Falahill Summit on 5 September 1963. In those days there were car factories in Scotland at Linwood near Paisley in the west and Bathgate near Edinburgh in the east, and in England at Halewood near Liverpool and in the Midlands. The last years of the Waverley route saw many car-train operations in both directions. The train shown here is a Bathgate–Oxford service carrying lorry chassis from the British Leyland plant. Rather strangely for this colliery, there is no sign of any steam 'pugs' fussing around.** Derek Cross

Above: **Class A3 Pacific No 60052 *Prince Palatine*, a Waverley-route regular, passes the exchange sidings with the National Coal Board near Newtongrange, on a northbound freight from Carlisle to Millerhill on 5 September 1963. The area immediately south of Edinburgh had a number of collieries, some of which were connected by rail to the Waverley route. Of the 78 Gresley 'A3s', 58 were fitted with German-style smoke-deflectors by BR towards the end of their working lives.** Derek Cross

Below: **Running tender-first near Newtongrange, 'J37' 0-6-0 No 64625 descends towards Millerhill Yard with a very uniformly loaded coal train in September 1963. The fireman, with a full tender and little or no more firing to do, appears very happy to be the centre of attention. The 'J37s' had been designed by Reid for the North British and were the most powerful 0-6-0s built for a Scottish railway. Reclassified from '4F' to '5F' in 1953, they were competent performers, especially on freight. No 64625 was built in 1921 and was not withdrawn until 1965, making it one of the last survivors of the pre-Grouping era.** Derek Cross

Left: **Another view of the southbound Millerhill–Carlisle mixed freight behind Class A3 Pacific No 60042** *Singapore* **on 9 May 1964, here pictured approaching Newtongrange station. This second photograph of the same train, just a few miles later, would have involved some of the famous Derek Cross 'train-chasing' driving!** Derek Cross

Below: **Class B1 4-6-0 No 61099 bowling along near Gorebridge with an Edinburgh–Carlisle semi-fast in summer 1964. After leaving Edinburgh Waverley these semi-fasts tended to stop at Eskbank, 8 miles into the journey. After some intermediate stations between there and Galashiels, they became all-stations. It was not a regular-interval service. This 'B1' was built by North British in Glasgow in 1946; it remained in traffic until September 1966 and was scrapped the following December.** Richard Barbour / Colour-Rail

Above: **The Gresley-designed 'D49' 'Shire'-class 4-4-0s were built at Darlington in the late 1920s. This one, No 62711 _Dumbartonshire_, is approaching Gorebridge station with an afternoon stopping train from Hawick to Edinburgh Waverley on 15 April 1961. It was withdrawn a month later, one of the last of the class to be withdrawn. Several of them worked these Waverley-route stopping trains for so long that more modern classes, excepting only a handful of BR-built Class 4 2-6-0s of the '76xx' series and the Class B1 4-6-0s, were kept at bay until the arrival of the diesels shortly before the closure of the route. 'D49' No 62712 _Morayshire_ is preserved at the Scottish Railway Preservation Society centre at Bo'ness.** Brian Stephenson

Below: **Class B1 4-6-0 No 61395 leaves Gorebridge station with an evening stopping train from Edinburgh to Hawick on 15 April 1961. The train is probably the 4.10pm from Waverley, which arrived at Hawick at 6.01pm — 1hr 50min for 53 miles! The departure time from Gorebridge (12 miles from Waverley) was 4.38pm, next stop Tynehead at 4.48pm. No 61395 was built by North British in 1952 and was withdrawn and cut up just 10 years later.** Brian Stephenson

Above: **A double-headed car train heading south for Halewood in Liverpool, pictured at Fushiebridge on Borthwick Bank between Gorebridge and Tynehead on the final part of the climb from Eskbank to Falahill, a distance of 10 miles at a ruling gradient of 1 in 70. The two Class 5 4-6-0s appear to be coping well with the 1 in 70 gradient, as might be expected given that only a single Ford Corsair can be seen on the otherwise empty wagons. The locomotives are Nos 44672 and 45120, both frequently seen on the Waverley route.** Richard Barbour / Colour-Rail

Below: **English Electric Type 4 diesel No D260 going well on Borthwick Bank with a lengthy mixed freight from Millerhill to Carlisle Kingmoor on 2 September 1965. One of an initial batch of seven such locomotives allocated new to the Scottish Region, No D260 had entered service in February 1960 and was destined to remain in normal traffic until January 1985.** John Spencer Gilks

Above: **A delightful 1950s wayside-station scene at Tynehead on 27 June 1956. A southbound stopping train to Carlisle arrives behind Class B1 4-6-0 No 61358, built at Darlington in October 1949. Note the anticipation on the platform, with children waiting to greet a parent, or perhaps set to board the train to the south.** Brian Stephenson

Below: **No 60037 *Hyperion* — the third Pacific to be built as an 'A3', in August 1934 at Doncaster — approaches Tynehead with an Edinburgh–Carlisle semi-fast in April 1961. Just 2 miles remain of the climb to Falahill (880 feet above sea level), the first summit encountered southbound from Edinburgh (the second being Whitrope, 46 miles distant). It will then be downhill for about 20 miles until a short section between Galashiels and Melrose is reached. *Hyperion* was withdrawn in December 1963.** Brian Stephenson

Top: **Passenger facilities at Tynehead were sparse, but they were kept neat and tidy. Here 'Peak' diesel No D24 races through the station on 2 September 1965 with the up 'Waverley' to London St Pancras via Carlisle, Settle and Leeds. The train left Edinburgh at 11.55am, made a first stop at Galashiels (12.41pm), continued via Carlisle (2.22pm), and will arrive at St Pancras at 9.17pm. Note the destination boards, just discernible above the windows of the two leading coaches. Renumbered 45 027, the locomotive remained in traffic until May 1981 and was eventually scrapped at Swindon Works in September 1983.** John Spencer Gilks

Above: **Pictured in the late summer of 1963 is Edinburgh St Margarets-allocated Class B1 4-6-0 No 61396 on a Carlisle–Edinburgh train at Falahill. As well as being the location of the first summit south of Edinburgh, this was essentially the point at which the railway ceased to be a suburban line through Midlothian and assumed the rural character that characterised it for the next 70 miles.** Derek Cross

Above: **Class A4 Pacific No 60031** *Golden Plover* heading south at Falahill Summit with an SLS special from Edinburgh to Carlisle in May 1965. In its latter years a Waverley-route regular, this locomotive would be one of the last 'A4s' to be withdrawn, in November 1965, yet it failed to escape the cutter's torch, being scrapped, unusually, at Campbell's of Renfrew early in 1966. Derek Cross

Below: Falahill Summit, in the Southern Uplands, was approached in both directions by fearsome gradients, the one to the north being marginally steeper. On 24 July 1965 a northbound mixed freight begins the descent towards Edinburgh Millerhill behind BR Class 9F No 92019 of Carlisle Kingmoor. The size and weight of the train will not have troubled this powerful 2-10-0. Built in 1954 at Crewe, this locomotive worked for fewer than 13 years, being withdrawn in 1967. Derek Cross

Above: **This picture, taken on 9 September 1968 at Stow, is of an unidentified Rail-blue-liveried English Electric Type 3 Co-Co on the 06.58 Hawick–Edinburgh train.** Not many pictures exist of these diesels (later Class 37s) on the Waverley route, for which they would probably have been ideal, equally at home on freight or passenger services. Although the route closed four months after the picture was taken, the '37s' have endured, with examples built in 1963 still in traffic today, 47 years later.
Andrew Muckley

Below: **A beautiful summer's day in May 1958 sees Class D30 4-4-0 No 62437 *Adam Woodcock* at the platform at Galashiels,** having arrived with an up local. Another locomotive is already attached to the other end of the train; it will make a leisurely return to Edinburgh later in the day. The 'D30s' were built at Cowlairs by the NBR in August 1915 and named after characters in Sir Walter Scott's novels. *Adam Woodcock*, one of the more conventionally named of the class, remained in traffic for only another month after the photograph was taken, when it was withdrawn after a working life of 43 years. Cyril Sanderson / Colour-Rail

Right: **Pictured in Galashiels station on 16 April 1965 is Gresley Class A4 Pacific No 60031 *Golden Plover*. The train is a Stephenson Locomotive Society (SLS) special from Edinburgh to Carlisle. With only five coaches, the 20 miles to Hawick and the following 11-mile climb to Whitrope Summit will not have presented any problem to the St Margarets-allocated locomotive, surprisingly sporting a yellow front number-plate.** Derek Cross

Below: **'Royal Scot' 4-6-0 No 46115 *Scots Guardsman* leaves Galashiels on 18 July 1965 with an Edinburgh Waverley–Carlisle stopper. The locomotive was withdrawn in December 1965, and some claim that this was the last time *Scots Guardsman* worked a passenger service for British Rail. After decades out of sight, one of the highlights of 2008 was its return to the main line.** Richard Barbour / Colour-Rail

Above: **The branch terminus at Selkirk in 1960. The branch
ran from Galashiels and normally saw a single-coach service
between the two stations. A consignment of new 'three-wheelers'
(as we knew them then) has just arrived, and the driver appears
to be inspecting these smart-looking machines. The locomotive is
Gresley Class V3 2-6-2T No 67606, which was built at Doncaster in
1930 as a 'V1' but was converted to a 'V3' in 1952 by increasing
the boiler pressure. Interestingly the class had been designed for
the Metropolitan lines, but they were never used on these or the
GNR suburban routes, instead spending much of their lives on
Tyneside and in Scotland.** A. J. Wickens

Below: **A northbound freight near Melrose on 22 August 1952.
The locomotive is Gresley Class K3 2-6-0 No 61882, built in 1929
at Doncaster. A total of 193 locomotives of this class were built;
they were excellent mixed-traffic machines, though gauge and
route availability were restricted by their large (6ft-diameter)
boilers. No 61882, which carried the early BR tender crest,
remained in traffic until December 1962.** Brian Stephenson

Above: **Class D49 'Shire' 4-4-0 No 62732**
***Dumfriesshire*, of 1928 vintage,**
passes Melrose signalbox in 1957
with a northbound train from Hawick to
Edinburgh. The locomotive carries a '68E'
(Carlisle Canal) shed plate. Towards the
end of steam Carlisle Canal was better
known as 12D, but from 1951 to early
1958 it had been a Scottish Region shed,
hence the '68E' code. Neville Stead

Right: **Thompson Class A2 Pacific No 60510**
***Robert the Bruce* enters Melrose station**
with a southbound Edinburgh–Carlisle
stopping train in the summer of 1957.
No 60510 was withdrawn from service
in November 1960. Today, the track bed
through the station is part of the Melrose
bypass, a two-lane road where there was
once a two-track main line. Neville Stead

Above: **A Class 08 diesel shunter, thought to be No D3890, crosses the impressive Leaderfoot Viaduct over the River Tweed on a dull day, 13 April 1965, with the branch goods to Greenlaw. This train left the Waverley route at Ravenswood Junction, between St Boswells and Melrose. Originally, this line went through to Duns and joined the East Coast main line at Reston, but this section** was closed as early as 1948, after a bridge was washed away near Greenlaw. By the time this picture was taken, the passenger service had long been withdrawn, and the freight service would last only three more months until 16 July 1965. **Pictures of this section are rare.** John Beckett

Above: **On 29 May 1964 BR Standard Class 2 No 78049 leaves Kelso on a train to St Boswells, which was the junction off the Waverley route, some 40 miles from Edinburgh. The ex-LNER brake coach probably did not have more than a single passenger on the 11-mile journey through the beautiful Roxburghshire** countryside, with stops at Roxburgh, Rutherford, Maxton and St Boswells, where the train terminated. At one stage the line had gone on east of Kelso to Coldstream and eventually Berwick-upon-Tweed, 35 miles from St Boswells. **The train ran five times a day, latterly on weekdays only.** John Spencer Gilks

Right: **A 'Peak' diesel, thought to be No D16, is pictured here near St Boswells on the morning Edinburgh–Carlisle train, on a dull 23 April 1965. Under the TOPS scheme, many diesels were renumbered in sequence, but the 'Peaks', which became Class 45, were not. However, in April 1974 No D16 was renumbered 45 016, being the only member of the class to retain some semblance of its original identity.**
John Beckett

Below: **Class D30 4-4-0 No 62440** *Wandering Willie* **had perhaps the best name in a class of classic names. It is seen here on the little locomotive shed at St Boswells on 19 May 1956. This small two-road shed was a sub-shed of Hawick, and the locomotives based there mainly worked on the branch to Berwick-upon-Tweed. Class V3 2-6-2T No 67606 is on the left of the picture, on the branch passenger train. No 62440 was built at Cowlairs in 1920 and withdrawn in August 1958. It was scrapped in 1960.**
John P. Wilson / Rail Archive Stephenson

Above: **Although spring has arrived, this picture, taken on 4 April 1961, still has the Border-country trees looking pretty bare. Class A3 Pacific No 60093 *Coronach* is pictured near St Boswells with the 9.20am Carlisle–Edinburgh train. The tall signalbox in the background was at the junction for the branch to Jedburgh and Kelso. *Coronach*, a Waverley-route stalwart based at Carlisle Canal, was withdrawn in May 1962.** Antony Linaker

Below: **Complete with headboard, the southbound 'Waverley' pulls away from St Boswells on 4 April 1961. Motive power was provided by Class A1 Pacific No 60159 *Bonnie Dundee*, built at Doncaster Works in November 1949. After leaving Edinburgh at 10.15, the train stopped first at Galashiels (11.05), then at Melrose (11.11) and St Boswells (11.17 to 11.19), and arrived at Hawick at 11.35. The 'Waverley' ran from June 1957 until September 1968, having succeeded the 'Thames–Forth Express' as the named train on the route. The corresponding service between St Pancras and Glasgow was called the 'Thames–Clyde Express' until, before it was abandoned entirely, it ceased to run south of Nottingham.** Antony Linaker

Above: **BRCW/Sulzer Type 2 diesel No D5311 has just passed Ravenswood Junction and approaches St Boswells with a train from Edinburgh to Carlisle on 26 August 1965. St Boswells, 40 miles from Edinburgh, had a junction on both sides of the station. To the north the branch diverged to Duns and eventually the ECML at Reston; to the south the junction was for the branches to Jedburgh and Kelso. No D5311, built at Smethwick in January 1959 and briefly allocated to Hornsey, still exists and is at present being restored at another English shed, Barrow Hill near Chesterfield.** Brian Stephenson

Below: **One day in Summer 1962, BR Standard Class 2 2-6-0 No 78047 and a single coach set off with a Kelso branch train across the Roxburgh Viaduct, which makes them look very small. Two trains a day ran from St Boswells, where the branch left the Waverley route, to Kelso and then on a further 24 miles to Berwick-upon-Tweed.** Richard Barbour / Colour-Rail

Left: **Having got over the shock of finding a named 'Jubilee' on the Jedburgh branch pick-up, the photographer gave chase. Here Stanier 'Jubilee' Class 6P5F 4-6-0 No 45696 *Arethusa* is pictured near Maxton, 3 miles from St Boswells, on the way back to the main Waverley route. With a reasonable load, the fireman has obliged with some smoke. It is May 1964; did the Carlisle shedmaster know that one of his 'Jubilees' was spending its time ambling about rural Roxburghshire?**
John Spencer Gilks

Below: **Norham is a wayside station between Berwick-upon-Tweed and Coldstream. This picture, taken on 20 July 1963, shows the St Boswells–Tweedmouth pick-up freight, which seems well used that day. The locomotive is Ivatt Class 2 2-6-0 No 46479, with the tall chimney, allocated at that time to Hawick shed after transfer from East Anglia. The small goods yard, the loading gauge and the signals all contribute to a typical post-war branch-line image. The distance from St Boswells to Tweedmouth was just under 35 miles.**
John Spencer Gilks

Above: **The author's expeditions with his father yielded something unexpected about once a year in terms of an unusual locomotive in an unusual place. One sunny afternoon in May 1964 it was the turn of John Spencer Gilks, who had gone to Jedburgh to photograph the twice-weekly pick-up goods. As he drove into the station yard, he was surprised to find named Stanier 'Jubilee' Class 6P5F 4-6-0 No 45696 *Arethusa* standing in the yard. This picture shows much of the station yard, with the shunting about to be completed.** John Spencer Gilks

Below: **The 11.24 St Boswells–Kelso sets off from St Boswells on 4 April 1961 behind BR Class 2-6-0 No 78046. Passing the tall and very recognisable Kelso Junction signalbox, the train is already on the branch line. The main Waverley route continues on the right. The train's consist is typical, being a brake coach and what appears to be a couple of horseboxes attached at the rear. The first stop will be Rutherford (the 11.24 did not call at the first station, Maxton), then Roxburgh, followed by Kelso, 11½ miles distant. No 78046 was built in 1955 at Darlington and had a working life of just over 10 years, being withdrawn in November 1966.** Antony Linaker

Above: **Kelso Junction on 4 April 1961 as BR Standard Class 2 2-6-0 No 78046 comes off the Kelso branch and joins the Waverley route just south of St Boswells station. The camera is facing south. The train is the 9.56am from Berwick-upon-Tweed to St Boswells via Coldstream and Kelso. This 35-mile journey from Berwick began in England, ran southwards to Tweedmouth, entered Scotland around Coldstream and continued on to Kelso and St Boswells.** Antony Linaker

Left: **September 1958 sees a spotless Class B1 4-6-0 No 61245 *Murray of Elibank* approaching Belses with an express for Carlisle. Belses, which is between St Boswells and Hawick, is 45 miles from Edinburgh, leaving 53 miles still to run to Carlisle. No 61245 was built by the North British Locomotive Company in Glasgow in 1947 and was withdrawn from service in July 1965.** Brian Morrison

Above: **Class B1 4-6-0 No 61099 drifts into Belses station with an Edinburgh–Carlisle train on 29 May 1964. The large station name board suggests alighting for two other villages: Ancrum, a couple of miles east on the A68 road, and Lilliesleaf, a mile or so west on the B6400.** John Spencer Gilks

Below: **Class A1 Pacific No 60121 *Silurian* is seen here in September 1964 with an Edinburgh semi-fast, thought to be the 1.40pm from Carlisle. It was due at Hawick at 3.08pm and would complete the 98 miles to Edinburgh at 4.34pm, having stopped thirteen times on the journey. The locomotive, built at Doncaster in December 1948, was then just 15 years old.**
Richard Barbour / Colour-Rail

Above: **Pictured near Hassendean in July 1965 is Stanier Class 5 4-6-0 No 45235, piloting a very dirty Gresley Class A4 Pacific No 60027 *Merlin*. This was indeed a rare combination. The load consists of new Ford Anglias from Ford at Halewood for the Scottish market, including what appears to be a single pink one! We saw earlier that car traffic in both directions was a feature of the last years of the Waverley route; less common on any line was a double-headed train featuring the finest locomotives from their designers Stanier and Gresley.** Richard Barbour / Colour-Rail

Below: **The then final Class A1 Pacific No 60162 *Saint Johnstoun* passes through Hassendean station on 15 April 1961. The train is a northbound service from Carlisle to Edinburgh Waverley, and is a typical consist of vans and passenger stock. Hassendean was a wayside station 4 miles north of Hawick; Belses would be the next station, followed by St Boswells.** Neville Stead

Above: **One of the 'Britannias' that were never allocated to a Carlisle shed was the** *doyen*, **No 70000** *Britannia*, **of Crewe North (5A) shed. It is seen here arriving in Hawick from the north on a mixed freight in the summer of 1962. Having been cascaded from the Eastern, Western and London Midland Regions, many of the 'Britannias' ended up based at Carlisle Kingmoor (12A) and became common on all the routes from the border into Scotland as the 1960s progressed. The Nith Valley route via Dumfries, the Clyde Valley route over Beattock and the Waverley route all saw these Pacifics.** Richard Barbour / Colour-Rail

Right: **On a wet day in the high summer of 1964, Standard Class 9F 2-10-0 No 92233 storms through the rain on a long mixed empty stock working, just north of Hawick. Not common on passenger work in Scotland, the '9Fs' did get to the Waverley route on freight, as well as being pressed into service on ECS movements, often on summer weekends. Some of the diesel classes had very short service lives, often because of mechanical shortcomings, but that was a charge that could not be levelled at the '9Fs'. But for the edict to end steam traction, they could have worked on into the 1980s. As it was, No 92233, built at Crewe in 1958, was withdrawn in February 1968, after less than 10 years' service.** Richard Barbour / Colour-Rail

Above: **BR Standard Class 2 2-6-0 No 78047 shunting at Hawick station in September 1964. Hawick saw trains start and terminate, and with the locomotive depot adjacent to the station there was always something going on. More than 40 years on there is, of course, no railway here any longer, but the site remains active as the large Teviotdale Leisure Centre.** Richard Barbour / Colour-Rail

Left: **Class A3 Pacific No 60068 *Sir Visto*, based at Carlisle Canal (68E) and a Waverley-route regular, departs from Hawick with a southbound express to Carlisle. A northbound freight occupies the northbound platform. The picture was taken in the mid-1950s, but the photographer noted that some wartime prefabricated houses ('prefabs', as they were known) could still be clearly seen on the hill in the background.** Neville Stead

Above: **Class A3 Pacific No 60079 *Bayardo*
is in the northbound platform at Hawick
station with an express for Edinburgh.
This early 1950s picture shows
'BRITISH RAILWAYS' still painted on the tender.
Perhaps this was a blue-liveried No 60079,
then allocated to Carlisle Canal, as it was
for many years. Hawick South signalbox
stands tall over the station, and an old
cattle wagon lurks in the yard on the right.**
Neville Stead

Right: **Class J36 0-6-0 No 65316 on station
pilot duty at Hawick on 23 July 1955,
which appears to be a fine summer's day.
With trains starting from and finishing at
Hawick, and parcels traffic and shunting in
the yard, the station pilot was an essential
part of the scene in the 1950s. No 65316
looks well for a locomotive already into its
56th year of work, having been built in
1899.** Brian Stephenson

Above: **Class A3 Pacific No 60041 *Salmon Trout* approaches Hawick station from the north with the up 'Thames–Forth' express on a fine summer's day on 27 June 1956. There are locomotives on shed on the left, and the station pilot, inevitably a Class J36 0-6-0, on the right.** *Salmon Trout* was not by any means a Waverley-route regular, being allocated to Haymarket at that time. The 'Thames–Forth' ran daily between Edinburgh Waverley and London St Pancras; there was never a headboard for this train, and it did not run officially after 1939. As with many railway matters, however, once a name is established it sticks! In 1957 what was effectively the same service was relaunched by BR as the 'Waverley'. Brian Stephenson

Below: **Pictured on a wet 30 May 1958 at Hawick is a southbound Edinburgh Waverley–Carlisle stopping train. Motive power is Class A2 Pacific No 60530 *Sayajirao*, named after the winner of the 1947 St Ledger. Hawick was just over halfway between Edinburgh and Carlisle. It was and is a major centre in the Borders, and reportedly there was always brisk passenger and freight activity. Most trains in steam days stopped at Hawick for five minutes or more, while the locomotives were watered, fires cleared and preparations made for the rigours ahead in both directions. The southward climb to Whitrope started at the end of the platform.** Brian Stephenson

Above: **Class V2 2-6-2 No 60965 at the platform at Hawick on 12 July 1958, with a northbound freight for Edinburgh. The next 19 miles to Galashiels would not be too demanding for a 'V2' on the Waverley route, but after leaving Melrose towards Galashiels it faced a more taxing second 19-mile stint in the form of the climb to Falahill. Built in 1943, No 60965 would remain in traffic until December 1962, being withdrawn after a working life of less than 20 years — unusually short for a 'V2'.** Brian Stephenson

Right: **A class not normally associated with the Waverley route is Gresley Class N2 0-6-2T, here represented by No 69510 on shed at Hawick, to which, for reasons that are unclear, it had recently been transferred from Parkhead shed (65C) in Glasgow. The locomotive is pictured in the smoky shed yard in the weak winter sunshine of 2 February 1959. It was built at Doncaster in 1921, and remained in traffic for another nine months after this picture was taken.** Neville Stead

Left: **Class B1 4-6-0 No 61357 is ready to depart southbound from Hawick towards Carlisle on 10 September 1959.** The picture shows the curved platform at Hawick, Hawick South signalbox in the background, and the locomotive depot and carriage sidings on the right. No 61357 is identifiable as an Edinburgh St Margarets locomotive both by the buffer-beam and by the '64A' shed plate attached over the 'SC' plate, which indicated a self-cleaning smokebox. Colin Hogg

Below: **Class D34 4-4-0 No 62488 *Glen Aladale* rests between jobs at Hawick MPD on 16 July 1960.** Built for the NBR at Cowlairs in 1920, *Glen Aladale* only had three months left in traffic, being withdrawn in October 1960 and scrapped in January 1961. The 'Glens' were built between 1913 and 1920. Many of them were scrapped at the BR works at Inverurie, north of Aberdeen, where, it is said, the cutters' cabin was adorned with a number of name-plates from 'Glens', which were painted on the splashers as opposed to being detachable plates. Neville Stead

Above: **Hawick shed yard, photographed from the platform on 16 July 1960, with a variety of classes and a variety of ages. BR Standard Class 2 2-6-0 No 78049 is five years old; Class J36 0-6-0 No 65317 behind it is 61 years old, and Class C16 4-4-2T No 67489 is 44 years old. The 'C16' was one of the last three of the class in service; it was withdrawn seven months later, in February 1961. The main building of the locomotive depot is behind No 78049.** Neville Stead

Below: **Gresley Class A4 Pacific No 60012** *Commonwealth of Australia*, **on a down train to Edinburgh, at Hawick station on 13 April 1961. Hawick station, with the locomotive shed (64G) straight across from the public platform, was an ideal 'spotting' location with much to see; in this picture one of the 'Shire' class is just visible on the right.** Antony Linaker

Above: **Here is an RCTS special, pictured at Hawick on 9 July 1961. This photograph features one of the four famous Scottish Region preserved pre-Grouping locomotives, the North British 4-4-0 No 256 *Glen Douglas*. Partnering the 'Glen' is Class J37 0-6-0 No 64624** on a return excursion to Tweedmouth and eventually Leeds. Sadly, no 'J37' was preserved from this class of 104 very successful freight locomotives, many of which worked for over 45 years, as did No 64624; however, the 'Glen' is now preserved at the SRPS Preservation Centre at Bo'ness. Gavin Morrison

Above right: **Pictured at Hawick station in June 1961 is Class D34 4-4-0 No 62484 *Glen Lyon*, which Hawick shed has deployed at short notice to cover the failure of a BR Class 4MT. The train is the 12.35pm local from Hawick to Carlisle. The driver is Jimmy Brand, who, as he had been brought up on these locomotives, fired back to Carlisle, allowing Peter Brock to drive. Peter remarked that "Jimmy knew how to get the best out of the 'Glen.'" No 62484 was withdrawn in December 1961.** Peter Brock

Right: **Pictured north of Hawick on 20 September 1961 is Standard Class 'Britannia' Pacific No 70018 *Flying Dutchman* with a Carlisle–Edinburgh semi-fast train. No 70018 was put into traffic on 25 June 1951 at Old Oak Common. It was moved first to Cardiff Canton and to Carlisle Canal in September 1961. The small tender and the hand-holds on the smoke-deflectors, replacing handrails, identify the locomotive as having come from the Western Region. No 70018 was transferred from Carlisle Canal in May 1962 and allocated to other sheds in England, including the other Carlisle sheds at Upperby and Kingmoor, before being scrapped in Scotland by the Motherwell Bridge Co. in May 1967. To have been allocated to all three sheds in Carlisle was most unusual, especially in a short 16-year life.** Neville Stead

Left: **The Waverley route had some fearsome gradients and some long climbs in both directions, through pretty unfriendly Border country where the weather could be dreadful at times, as this March 1962 picture confirms. In Scotland there is a very good local word used to describe such days — 'dreich' — which fits the bill in this shot. Class A2 Pacific No 60519 *Honeyway* accelerates away from Hawick station with a southbound freight. Eleven unrelenting miles, much of it at steeper than 1 in 100, lie ahead through Stobs and Shankend before the summit, Whitrope, is reached. The weather would probably be even worse here! No 60519 remained in service for only nine more months, being withdrawn in December 1962.** Neville Stead

Left: **Pictured on the Teviot Viaduct at the south end of Hawick station is Class A2 Pacific No 60530 *Sayajirao*, another Waverley-route regular. This fine close-up shows one of the last fifteen locomotives of Thompson design, in fact a redesign by Thompson's successor, Arthur Peppercorn, who became CME of the LNER in 1946. Although classified 'A2', there were detail differences between these and the original locomotives; the cylinders were further forward and the wheelbase was 2ft 6in smaller. No 60530 was built in Doncaster in 1948 and withdrawn at the end of 1966 from Dundee shed.** Neville Stead

Above: **Class A3 Pacific No 60052 *Prince Palatine* on Stobs Viaduct in May 1963 with a fitted freight from Edinburgh to Carlisle Kingmoor. The photographer's Ford Prefect car adds to the 1960s feel.** Richard Barbour / Colour-Rail

Below: **An empty stock train from Riccarton Junction to Hawick, at Acreknowe, near Stobs army camp, on a sunny evening in July 1963. The switched-out signalbox at Stobs Camp can be seen in the distance. Not unusually, the train is hauled by a BRCW/Sulzer Type 2 diesel. This one is unidentified.** John Spencer Gilks

Above: **Class A1 Pacific No 60121 *Silurian* near Stobs Camp on a very pleasant evening in September 1964. The train is a down semi-fast service from Carlisle to Edinburgh Waverley, with which the Pacific appears to be coping well. *Silurian* was built at Doncaster in December 1948 and remained in traffic for just one more year, being withdrawn in October 1965.** Richard Barbour / Colour-Rail

Below: **By October the nights in the Border country are beginning to draw in. Pictured in October 1964 near Stobs Camp, just before the sun disappears, is Gresley Class V2 2-6-2 No 60813, with the modified chimney, working hard with a heavy southbound freight from Millerhill to Kingmoor. The 11 miles from the end of the platform at Hawick to Whitrope Summit averaged 1 in 75.** Richard Barbour / Colour-Rail

Right: **Fitted with German-style smoke-deflectors, Class A3 Pacific No 60052 *Prince Palatine* storms up the ruling 1-in-80 gradient past Stobs in October 1964, with a southbound freight to Carlisle Kingmoor. The yellow stripe on the cab side denotes that the locomotive is barred from working under lines electrified at 25kV. Built at Doncaster in 1924 as an 'A1', *Prince Palatine* remained in traffic until January 1966, one of the last 'A3s' to be withdrawn.** Richard Barbour / Colour-Rail

Below right: **On a long train of empty wagons, Class A2 Pacific No 60530 *Sayajirao* is working hard past Stobs Camp, about halfway through the climb from Hawick to Whitrope Summit. The train is a southbound service from Millerhill Yard and has completed about 57 miles of the 98-mile route between Edinburgh and Carlisle. The 1948-built *Sayajirao* was a regular Waverley-route performer in the 1960s, until its withdrawal in November 1966.** Richard Barbour / Colour-Rail

Top: **Stobs station was a rural affair, seen here on 27 May 1963 as a passenger train from Carlisle rolls into the wayside station behind another unidentified BRCW/Sulzer Type 2 diesel. Stobs was a remote place, known in railway terms principally for its proximity to the army camp.** John Spencer Gilks

Above: **Stobs is just under halfway between Hawick and the summit at Whitrope, 11 miles of unrelenting climb. On a short freight from Millerhill to Carlisle, BR 'Britannia' Pacific No 70001 *Lord Hurcomb* appears to be going well in June 1965. No 70001 was placed in traffic on 14 February 1951, first as an express passenger locomotive on the Great Eastern out of Liverpool Street. It was later transferred to Willesden, then Aston, before ending up at Carlisle Kingmoor in October 1964. It was withdrawn in August 1966.** John Spencer Gilks

Right: **A pair of unidentified BRCW/Sulzer Type 2 diesels, one on a passenger train, the other on a freight, passing each other near Stobs Camp in Autumn 1961. By 1962 half the stopping services over the Waverley route had been taken over by these 1,160hp machines. They coped well with the Waverley route and generally kept good time on passenger trains that might stop at more than 20 intermediate stations.** Peter Brock

Below: **Class V2 2-6-2 No 60931 near Shankend on a down freight in June 1961. Also of interest are the platelayers and gangers maintaining the already pristine permanent way. The wheelbarrow was part of their maintenance tool kit — those were the days!** Malcolm Thompson / Colour-Rail

Above: **Imagine a commuting journey like this! The 6.13pm stopping train from Carlisle to Hawick is pictured crossing the viaduct at Shankend, 7 miles from its destination. Due to leave Shankend at 7.27pm, the train would arrive at Hawick at 7.40pm. It is hauled by Standard Class 4 2-6-4 No 80122, which was built in faraway Brighton in August 1955.** Richard Barbour / Colour-Rail

Left: **Near Shankend on 23 April 1965, Class V2 2-6-2 No 60931 struggles with the gradient, the weather and the endless curves on the Waverley route. Here the climb to Whitrope stiffens to 1 in 75 for the last 3 miles to the tunnel, easing to 1 in 95 through the tunnel itself before reaching Whitrope signalbox, which marked the summit. This wheezing locomotive survived only another five months in traffic before being withdrawn in September 1965.** John Beckett

Right: **This southbound train from Edinburgh Waverley to Carlisle is hauled by Class A3 Pacific No 60099 *Call Boy*. The date is 12 August 1961, the Glorious Twelfth, the start of the year's grouse-shooting, for which there is plenty of scope in these remote hills. As well as the exhaust note of the Waverley-route trains, the hills around Shankend are probably alive with the sound of gunshots on that day.** Brian Stephenson

Below: **With its 15 arches, the graceful 600ft-long Shankend Viaduct is one of the most striking on the whole Waverley route, immediately north of the wayside Shankend station. In this picture it is being crossed by the northbound 'Waverley', headed by Class A3 No 60041 *Salmon Trout*, in mid-1961. By now *Salmon Trout* had been fitted with a double chimney but not yet with German-style smoke-deflectors, which it acquired in early 1963. The locomotive remained in traffic until November 1965 and was then taken to Cowlairs Works in Glasgow, where reportedly it was cannibalised to keep preserved 'A3' No 4472 *Flying Scotsman* running.** Antony Linaker

Left: **An unusual view of a freight train headed by a Class V2 2-6-2, this 1961 photograph was taken near Shankend from a brake van and also captures the ruggedness of the area around Whitrope Summit.** Peter Brock

Below: **Peppercorn Class A1 Pacific No 60159 *Bonnie Dundee* at the head of a six-coach semi-fast from Carlisle to Edinburgh Waverley in the early 1960s. The locomotive does not seem to be having any sort of struggle on the climb to Whitrope, some 1006 feet above sea level, and now no more than 2 miles away. After Riccarton the next station stop will be Shankend, followed by Stobs. *Bonnie Dundee* was a Waverley-route regular when this picture was taken.** Peter Brock

Above: **The 2.36pm train from Edinburgh to Carlisle on 13 April 1961, just starting the descent from Whitrope towards Riccarton Junction and eventually Carlisle. The signalbox can be seen in the distance. The train is hauled by Class A1 Pacific No 60159 *Bonnie Dundee* — superpower for the five-coach load.**
Antony Linaker

Below: **Class B1 4-6-0 No 61290 raises an echo around the Roxburghshire hills on the long 1-in-75 grind towards the summit at Whitrope. The train is the 11.40 Carlisle–Galashiels goods, and appears well loaded on this Friday towards the end of May 1961. No 61290 was built by North British in early 1948 and was withdrawn by March 1962, less than a year after this picture was taken.** Peter Brock

Above: **Class V2 2-6-2 No 60840 reaches the top of the long northbound climb at Whitrope on 8 July 1961. The train is a down freight heading for Edinburgh Niddrie Yard. Class V2s were common on the Waverley route through the 1950s and until 1962, but their demise thereafter was very rapid. All 184 examples built** were active at the end of 1961, but by the end of 1963 only 72 remained, and by the end of 1965 only 14. One of them, the pioneer *Green Arrow*, survives in preservation at the National Railway Museum at Shildon. Gavin Morrison

Left: **July 1961 saw the West Riding branch of the RCTS run a special from Leeds to Hawick to Tweedmouth, and back via Newcastle. 'Duchess' Pacific No 46247 _City of Liverpool_ started the day from Leeds to Carlisle; then two Class B1 4-6-0s, No 61290 and No 61242 _Alexander Reith Gray_, pictured here at Whitrope Summit, took the train from Carlisle to Hawick. _Glen Douglas_ and a Class J37 0-6-0 then proceeded to Tweedmouth before going back to Leeds. That probably all cost less than £5 in 1961!**
Gavin Morrison

Above: **Class A1 Pacific No 60162 _Saint Johnstoun_ leaves Whitrope Tunnel with the 2.30pm Edinburgh Waverley–Carlisle train in the spring of 1962. It is here at Whitrope that the nascent Waverley Route Heritage Association was established in 2001, and now has a locomotive and collection of rolling stock. The author wishes this group every success.**
Brian Stephenson

Right: **Class 5 4-6-0 No 45195 passes the signalbox at Whitrope (or Whitrope Siding, to give it its full and proper title). The train is an Edinburgh–Carlisle freight, seen at the summit before beginning the descent southward through Riccarton and the south.**
Brian Stephenson

Above and left: **The early part of 1963 was one of the hardest winters in recent times, and even now, nearly 50 years on, it is still mentioned for its severity. The Waverley route was badly affected by snow, and two freight trains were trapped early in January. Between 6 January and 9 January Class A2 Pacific No 60535** *Hornets Beauty* **was stranded in a snowdrift between Whitrope and Riccarton. As can be seen, it was simply left where it had given up the struggle, until the plough got through to both open the line and recover the Pacific. Carlisle Canal put together three locomotives, Class 4F 0-6-0 No 44081, 'Black Five' 4-6-0 No 45103 and Ivatt Class 4 2-6-0 No 43138 to help to reopen the Waverley route from the southern end. Eventually, single-line working was restored, the locomotive was recovered, and gradually the Waverley route got back to normal. The locomotive had been working an Aberdeen–Carlisle freight when, reportedly, the train ran into 16ft snowdrifts. Such was the depth of snow and the degree of freezing that dynamite had to be used to move it. Needless to say, the consignment of whisky was one of the first traffics to be rescued. No 60535's winter holiday at Whitrope did no lasting damage; in fact, the locomotive was amongst the last half-dozen of the class to be withdrawn in mid-1965.**
Peter Brock (both)

Above: **The snow-ploughing team pauses near Whitrope Summit in January 1963. Peter Brock was among the Carlisle crews that turned out, and had his camera with him to record the rescue mission. The '4F' No 44081 had the snowplough attached. In the background the tops of the snow fences can be seen, but such was the volume of snow that even they proved ineffective.** Peter Brock

Below: **Another picture taken in January 1963 during the big freeze. The scene is probably in the Steele Road/Riccarton/Whitrope area, but the exact location is unclear. The train is a short freight, perhaps coal for the signalboxes, and is hauled by BR Standard Class 4 2-6-0 No 76050.** Peter Brock

Above: **Here we see Peter Brock himself on this memorable occasion.** Peter Brock collection

Above: **Class D20 4-4-0 No 62387 awaits departure from the bay platform at Riccarton Junction with a train for Hexham on 3 July 1954. The Border Counties line to Hexham was closed some years before the Waverley route, and a paragraph extracted from the summer 1963 Scottish Region timetable describes the alternative arrangements as follows: 'The passenger train service between Riccarton and Hexham has been withdrawn. Omnibus services operated by Norman Fox depart from Steele Road on Mondays and Saturdays only at 10.15am and 5.00pm serving Deadwater, Kielder Forest, Lewiefield, Plashetts, Falstone, Thorneyburn, Tarset and Bellingham. Charlton Buses (Mid-Tyne Transport) provide connecting services at Bellingham for intermediate places to Hexham'. Note the reference to Mondays *and* Saturdays, not Mondays *to* Saturdays.** Brian Stephenson

Left: **The main Waverley route can be seen on the far right of this 1961 picture of the Border Counties line from Hexham. Class J39 0-6-0 No 64888 is pictured arriving at Riccarton Junction from the Hexham direction with a train of what appears to be mainly cattle wagons. For a time after the line from Hexham was closed, this end of the line was used for the storage of such wagons.** Peter Brock

Above: **Haymarket (64A) Class B1 4-6-0 No 61221 *Sir Alexander Erskine-Hill* approaches Riccarton Junction from the south with a mixed freight from Carlisle to Millerhill Yard in Edinburgh on a glorious summer day in 1963. The 'B1' appears to be going well as the fireman looks out from the cab before the final 2 miles to Whitrope Summit.** Peter Brock

Below: **English Electric 2000hp Type 4 diesel No D262 awaits the 'right away' from Riccarton Junction on 9 September 1968, just four months before the Waverley route closed. The train is an Edinburgh–Carlisle service and includes a blue-and-grey coach** in the formation. Riccarton Junction station had first opened for traffic in October 1862, as the junction for the Border Counties line to Hexham from the Waverley route. It was possible to access this little railway community (only about 100 people lived there) only by rail, with food and provisions arriving from the Co-op in Hawick each day. No D262, later No 40 062, was new to Edinburgh Haymarket shed in March 1960. Having been withdrawn from Carlisle Kingmoor in November 1981, the locomotive was scrapped at Swindon Works in May 1983. Andrew Muckley

Above: **In May 1961 Haymarket-allocated Class A3 Pacific No 60090 *Grand Parade* has just left lonely Riccarton Junction (the houses are visible top right) on the falling 1 in 75 gradient. The final 33 miles to Carlisle are all more-or-less downhill, so the hard work for the fireman is over. The train is a Dundee–Carlisle fast freight.** Peter Brock

Below: **Motherwell Class 5 4-6-0 No 45309 has been commandeered by Carlisle Canal in August 1961 to work an 8.45am fast goods from Carlisle to Niddrie. Pictured approaching Riccarton Junction, with the much-photographed bridge in the background, the train appears to be making good progress on the climb towards Whitrope Summit. No 45309 was built by Armstrong-Whitworth in January 1937, and remained in traffic for almost 30 years until September 1966.** Peter Brock

Above: **The last day on the Waverley route, 5 January 1969, sees English Electric 'Deltic' Type 5 No D9007 *Pinza* at the northbound platform at Riccarton Junction with one of the 'last-day' specials, the RCTS 'West Riding' from Leeds to Edinburgh. Unusually for the Waverley route, the train is made up of air-braked stock.** Gavin Morrison

Right: **Carlisle Canal-allocated Class J39 0-6-0 No 64899 at Riccarton Junction in May 1963 with the Hawick–Carlisle pick-up goods. This was the locomotive's final run before it was withdrawn and ultimately broken up.** Peter Brock

Left: **Class A3 Pacific No 60068 *Sir Visto*, seen from the footplate of another Class A3 Pacific, the unique No 60097 *Humorist*, as the trains cross near Riccarton Junction in June 1961. *Sir Visto* is heading north with a passenger train for Carlisle; *Humorist* is plugging away with a fast goods from Carlisle to Niddrie Yard. As can be seen, No 60097 was fitted with a different type of smoke-deflector from the German style. It was the only 'A3' to have them, and also a double chimney, before 1958.** Peter Brock

Below: **The driver's view from the footplate of Class V2 2-6-2 No 60887 as it climbs past Riccarton South signalbox on the 2.42pm Carlisle Canal–Aberdeen fast goods in April 1961. The 'V2' is clearly working hard on the 1 in 75 section, which started 8 miles earlier and still has 2 miles of the climb to Whitrope ahead. As shown in a number of these footplate pictures, the tidiness of the permanent way was a credit to all concerned, evidence perhaps that a greater pride in the job was taken 50 years ago.** Peter Brock

Right: **Arnton Fell dominates the horizon above the Waverley route, as seen in August 1961 from the fireman's side of Class V2 2-6-2 No 60971. The train is a Niddrie–Carlisle freight. It is approaching the bridge at Riccarton Junction from the north, having conquered both summits — first Falahill and then Whitrope — and with only the downhill run to Carlisle yet to come.** Peter Brock

Below: **An up Edinburgh–Carlisle stopping train is pictured near Steele Road in May 1964. Motive power is provided by an unidentified BRCW/Sulzer Type 2 diesel. These 'locals' took 2hr 53min for the 98-mile journey with between 13 and 15 station stops. This gave an average speed of 34 mph.** John Spencer Gilks

Above: **A pair of Class 17 Clayton diesels, No D8601 and No D8606, is seen near Steele Road in the high summer of 1965 on an enormously long train. By this time both Millerhill and Kingmoor yards had become fully operational, even as wagon-load traffic started to decline rapidly. That day a large number of vans had been found, and the two locomotives, then both one year old, were entrusted with the service to Carlisle. They are both in BR green livery. A few of the class survived long enough to acquire Rail blue, but these two did not last long in traffic, for they were withdrawn in 1971. It was No D8606 that hauled the last freight over the Waverley route, a Hawick–Millerhill trip working on 25 January 1969.** Derek Cross

Left: **St Margarets-allocated Class B1 No 61307 is pictured working hard near Steele Road with the 8.40am Carlisle– Niddrie fitted freight on what looks like a fine April day in 1960. The gradient at this point is a steady 1 in 75 for around 9 miles from Newcastleton through Steele Road and Riccarton to the summit just before Whitrope Tunnel.** Peter Brock

Above: **In this June 1960 picture, Class A2 Pacific No 60530** *Sayajirao* **is between Newcastleton and Steele Road on the climb to Whitrope. The train is the 1.40pm Carlisle–Edinburgh Waverley, due at Steele Road at 2.31pm and with an Edinburgh arrival time of 4.32pm. Pictures taken in this area show that it was quite wooded, unlike the scenery further up the line, which was very bleak. Since the line closed, some seriously large commercial forestry projects have emerged throughout the area, an extension of the nearby Kielder Forest.** Peter Brock

Below: **The 3.22pm Carlisle–Edinburgh Waverley train leaves Steele Road, about halfway up the climb from Newcastleton to Whitrope, on 13 April 1961. The short train is not a problem for Class A1 Pacific No 60162** *Saint Johnstoun*, **then the last of the class of 49 locomotives, all built at Doncaster in British Railways days between August 1948 and December 1949, albeit to an LNER design. The first of the class, No 60113** *Great Northern*, **had been built much earlier, and when added to the 'new' locomotives gave an operating fleet of 50. None survived into preservation.** Antony Linaker

Above: **An unidentified 'Peak' diesel passes Steele Road with the down 'Waverley' from London St Pancras to Edinburgh Waverley (1S64) on 28 May 1964. The train left St Pancras at 9.15am, calling at Nottingham, Chesterfield, Sheffield, Rotherham Masborough, Leeds City, Skipton, Hellifield Settle and Appleby before reaching Carlisle at 3.54pm. Thereafter the train called at Newcastleton, Hawick, St Boswells, Melrose and Galashiels, arriving at Edinburgh Waverley at 6.34 pm. At that time the 'Waverley' was one of 13 Anglo-Scottish named trains listed in a special 'blue pages' section of the Scottish Region timetable.** John Spencer Gilks

Below: **Class A3 Pacific No 60103** *Flying Scotsman* **was not a regular sight on the Waverley route in its BR days, which ended in January 1963. Once sold to Alan Pegler, however, the locomotive began to travel away from the East Coast main line, and here, on 25 June 1966, it is pictured at Steele Road, back in its LNER livery as No 4472. The train is a Warwickshire Railway Society special carrying the 'Aberdonian' headboard and running between London Waterloo and Aberdeen. On enthusiast specials there are always a number of people looking out of the windows, but the two gentlemen in the second coach appear intent on falling out of the train!** Derek Cross

Top: **A pair of Clayton Type 1 diesels, No D8570 followed by D8578, on an afternoon freight from Carlisle Kingmoor to Millerhill, seen here at Steele Road on 25 June 1966. Placed in traffic in January 1964, these were still fairly new locomotives and should not have been emitting steam-engine quantities of black smoke; setting the 'Claytons' to work on the steeply graded Waverley route was perhaps not a good idea. Both the locomotives shown would be withdrawn by the end of the decade.** Derek Cross

Above: **The normal monotony of the Waverley-route semi-fast stock is broken by the inclusion of a blue-and-grey coach towards the back of this five-coach, four-van formation photographed at Steele Road on 26 June 1966. The train is a Carlisle–Edinburgh Waverley service, and the power is provided by BRCW/Sulzer Type 2 No D5304. The wisps of steam between the carriages betray that the steam heating is on and working, even though the longest day of the year had fallen earlier in the week.** Derek Cross

Left: **An entry in the 1963 timetable, outlining the somewhat minimal replacement bus arrangements after the Border Counties line to Hexham closed, has already been quoted. In this picture from 10 September 1968, it will be seen that from 8 July that year that even the bus service had been cancelled. Alongside the blackboard is a British Railways poster advising that from 27 March 1967, Steele Road and other stations would be unstaffed, and tickets would be obtainable from the guard on the train. It seemed almost inevitable that the Waverley route would not last much longer; and so it came about, the last trains running in January 1969.** Andrew Muckley

Below: **The 7.06am Edinburgh Waverley–Carlisle train pulls into the remote station at Steele Road at around 9.20am on 10 September 1968. Motive power is provided, unusually, by two-tone green BR/Sulzer Type 2 diesel No D5068. New in December 1959 to March depot in East Anglia, it was later transferred to Haymarket depot in Edinburgh and was withdrawn in October 1972.** Andrew Muckley

Above: **Peter Brock had not been firing for long when one day in 1960 his Class B1 4-6-0 No 61239 became derailed. This happened when they were on a permanent way job in the yard at Newcastleton when, according to Peter, the road spread beneath the locomotive. They could not re-rail the 'B1', so the breakdown crane from Carlisle Kingmoor had to be called out. Not unusually** for Kingmoor, they 'borrowed' a locomotive, this time another **Class B1, No 61038 *Blacktail*, from Neville Hill shed in Leeds. There was much ribbing from the other Canal men, and much embarrassment for Peter and his driver, but it all ended well and without damage, as this picture of the two locomotives shows.**
Peter Brock

Above left: **A very short pick-up goods at Newcastleton in June 1964. Headed by Ivatt Class 4 2-6-0 No 43045, the working also involved the Langholm branch. By 1964 volumes were dropping as rail traffic transferred to road. The locomotive was built at Horwich Works in October 1949, and remained in traffic only until 1966.** L. Williamson / Colour-Rail

Left: **Storming away from the Newcastleton stop, the 9.20am Carlisle–Edinburgh Waverley is already into the climb to the summit at Whitrope. The train is hauled by Class A2 Pacific No 60535 *Hornets Beauty*. Newcastleton was quite a large station and served an extensive hinterland. It was also the station that hosted a major protest the day the line closed in January 1969, when reportedly over 200 people turned out to delay the Edinburgh–London St Pancras sleeper by more than two hours.** Peter Brock

Top: **This northbound freight has just swept through Newcastleton at speed in order to get a good run at the bank up to Whitrope. The train is the 2.42pm Carlisle–Aberdeen fast goods via Niddrie in Edinburgh, and comprises 46 single vans. The motive power on this August day in 1960 is provided by Gresley Class A3 Pacific No 60087 *Blenheim*, which was built at Doncaster in April 1930 and remained in traffic until October 1963.** Peter Brock

Above: **A Carlisle–Edinburgh Waverley train in the station at Kershopefoot on 25 February 1967. Since about 1964 these semi-fast workings had been in the hands of the BRCW/Sulzer Type 2s, but on this occasion the train is headed by Class 5 4-6-0 No 44792, which was substituting for a failure. No 44792 would be withdrawn seven months later.** Gavin Morrison

Above: **The first of Gresley's Class A3 Pacifics, No 60035**
Windsor Lad, **seen near Kershopefoot during the summer of 1961**
with the 9.20am Carlisle–Edinburgh Waverley. *Windsor Lad*
was built at Doncaster in July 1934 and remained in service
until September 1961, when it was scrapped almost immediately.
The double chimney was fitted in early 1959, but this locomotive
never received the German-style smoke-deflectors. Peter Brock

Below: **Class A3 Pacific No 60037** *Hyperion* **near Kershopefoot**
with an Edinburgh–Carlisle train in 1961. This stopping train does
not have any vans, but it does have a very mixed rake of stock;
the first two vehicles look fairly old. Kershopefoot, 21 miles
north of Carlisle, is in a dip between Newcastleton and Penton.
The modest station had two side platforms, a signalbox and a
level crossing. Its main claim to fame is that it was more or less
on the Scotland–England border. It was indeed the last station
in England on the Waverley route; Newcastleton, the next station,
was the first in Scotland. Peter Brock

Right: **After dealing with the less-severe gradients between Kershopefoot and Newcastleton, 4 miles from Steele Road, Claytons Type 1 diesels Nos D8570 and D8578 are not looking well prepared for the coming 12 miles to the summit at Whitrope, at the ruling gradient of 1 in 75. The date is 25 June 1966, and the pair is seen on page 93 at Steele Road on the same occasion; the train was moving so slowly that the photographer was able to get two pictures — still no mean feat when the geometry of the roads on that part of the Waverley route is considered.** Derek Cross

Below: **Class 5 4-6-0 No 44792 arrives at Kershopefoot station with a Carlisle–Edinburgh train on 25 February 1967.** Gavin Morrison

Left: **Taken from the footplate of Class J39 0-6-0 No 64892 near Penton, this photograph shows Heaton-allocated (52B) Class V2 2-6-2 No 60945 heading the 6.40am Edinburgh Waverley–Carlisle train. The passenger train has about 16 miles to run to Carlisle, where it is due to arrive at 9.58am. The timetable of the day showed a connection at Carlisle for London Euston, due to arrive at 3.45pm. After the Penton stop the train would call at Riddings Junction and then Longtown, followed by Carlisle. The freight behind the Class J39 is a permanent-way train heading for Riccarton.** Peter Brock

Below: **In this view from the footbridge at Riddings Junction station in June 1960, the branch to Langholm, the small yard and the Waverley-route main line are all clearly visible. Of note from this high vantage-point is the pristine condition of the permanent way and platforms. Class A2 Pacific No 60535 *Hornets Beauty* is arriving with an Edinburgh–Carlisle train on the main line while Class J39 0-6-0 No 64932 is about to set off for Langholm. No 64932, which looks healthy, had just a month left in traffic.** John Spencer Gilks

Above: **Class A3 Pacific No 60041 *Salmon Trout* sets off southbound from Riddings Junction with the 6.40am semi-fast train from Edinburgh Waverley to Carlisle in May 1961. With just the stop at Longtown to come, the train is about 25 minutes away from its destination.** Peter Brock

Below: **A pair of Waverley-route regulars is pictured here in Riddings Junction station in 1961. Class A3 Pacific No 60093 *Coronach* is arriving with a Carlisle–Edinburgh Waverley train. It will make a connection with the Langholm branch train waiting at the adjacent platform behind Class J39 0-6-0 No 64884. This wonderful picture is typical of the scenes on the Waverley route.** John Spencer Gilks

Left: **Class A3 Pacific No 60068 *Sir Visto*
at Riddings Junction with the 9.10am train
to Edinburgh Waverley, summer 1961.
Riddings Junction appears to have been
known locally as 'the Moat', for reasons
that it has not been possible to establish.
In railway terms, it was the junction for
Langholm, and the viaduct in the
background was on that branch. *Sir Visto*
was one of Carlisle Canal's four Class A3s
(the others being Nos 60079, 60093 and
60095). Built as an 'A1', it was later
reclassified 'A10' and was the only member
of that class to be taken into BR stock,
finally being rebuilt as an 'A3' in December
1948.** Peter Brock

Below: **On 13 June 1964, Ivatt Class 4 2-6-0
No 43139 awaits departure at Langholm
station with the 3.30pm (Fridays only)
to Carlisle. Although there is a van or two
in the yard, the goods shed door is closed,
indicating not much use. This train to
Carlisle, joining the Waverley route at
Riddings Junction, would take 53 minutes
for the 21-mile journey.** John Spencer Gilks

Top: **The 10.10am from Langholm to Carlisle crossing Gilnockie Viaduct in June 1961. More usual motive power for the Langholm branch was the ex-LNER Class J39 0-6-0s and later the Ivatt Class 4 2-6-0s, so Fowler Class 4 2-6-4T No 42317, seen here, was a rare visitor. It was a Carlisle Canal locomotive, built for the Midland Railway at Derby in 1928. Although only 7 miles long, the Langholm branch crossed the border between England and Scotland, Langholm being in Dumfriesshire.** Peter Brock

Above: **Waverley regular Class J39 0-6-0 No 64884 is pictured again on the Langholm branch in 1961, standing in the small terminus station ready to leave with a branch train to Riddings Junction, there to connect with the main-line trains. The run-round arrangements at Langholm were unusual, as the train had to propel out of the platform, run round and then propel back into the platform. Also of note here is the rather leisurely loading of what appears to be loose coal from the wagons to a road vehicle. The site is now a housing estate.** Neville Stead

Above: **The 6.22am Langholm–Carlisle behind Ivatt Class 4 2-6-0 No 43139, heading towards Riddings Junction on 13 April 1961. Derek always used to say that shortly before a branch line was closed, money would always be spent on it! Here on the Langholm branch, less than 3 years before closure, new fencing has very obviously appeared. The passage of the train has disturbed the local chickens. The passenger service ceased from 13 June 1964.** Antony Linaker

Below: **Class J39 0-6-0 No 64884 crossing Riddings Viaduct with the Langholm branch train in August 1961. Peter Brock remarked that working the Langholm branch passenger trains with Class J39s running tender-first was a hair-raising experience. It involved tearing around the tight downhill curves and across the viaduct at speeds of more than 40mph. Dust flew from the tender into the cab, the big ends of the 1935-built locomotive rattling about below the firebox. Carlisle Canal-based No 64884 was a Langholm branch regular until it was withdrawn in March 1962.** Peter Brock

Above: **In August 1961 Fowler 2-6-4T No 42317 pauses at Gilnockie station with a train for Langholm. Gilnockie for Clay Gate, to give the station its full name, was not quite 3 miles from Riddings Junction, Langholm being 4 miles further on. Most trains connected with Waverley-route trains at Riddings Junction, though there were two direct return trains between Langholm and Carlisle each day.**
Peter Brock

Right: **Peter Brock rarely went anywhere without his camera. Pictured from the fireman's side of Class J39 0-6-0 No 64892, Class V2 2-6-2 No 60980 heads towards the camera on a southbound fitted freight for Carlisle Yard. The picture was taken near Scots Dyke in spring 1961. Peter Brock always felt that the 'J39s' were very rough-riding locomotives, so an image as sharp as this represented a very good effort.**
Peter Brock

Above: **In May 1961, Edinburgh St Margarets-allocated Class V2 2-6-2 No 60882 rolls downhill near Scots Dyke on the falling grade from Penton towards Riddings Junction, which was the next station on the line. The final stop will be Longtown before the train terminates at Carlisle. This is the early morning passenger train from Edinburgh Waverley to Carlisle, which left at 6.40am.** Peter Brock

Below: **A Langholm–Carlisle local train at Longtown on 19 June 1958. The train is hauled by Class J39 0-6-0 No 64733, a product of Darlington in 1927. The Langholm-branch service to/from Carlisle, comprising seven trains a day in each direction (some direct, others requiring a change at Riddings Junction) was leisurely, to say the least, an average of about 55 minutes being allowed for the journey of 7 miles from Langholm to Riddings Junction and 14 miles thence to Carlisle.** Derek Cross

Right: **This is the closest the author could find to a photograph of Lyneside. Seen between Lyneside and Longtown, the train is a northbound goods for Millerhill behind Class V2 2-6-2 No 60970, strolling along one of the few flat sections south of Longtown. After Longtown there is a short section of 1 in 100 to Scotchdyke; then it is flat again to just before Riddings Junction; then it is almost all climb to Whitrope, 22 miles in all. The 'V2s' were excellent locomotives, credited with helping the war effort and one of the few classes that continued to be built during the war, No 60970 being completed at Darlington in May 1943. They were equally at home on passenger or freight on the Waverley route.** Derek Cross

Below: **The bright morning of 16 July 1965 sees a workers' train travelling from Carlisle to Harker, for the large military site there. Harker was the first station out of Carlisle on the Waverley route, being about halfway (just under 5 miles) between Carlisle Citadel and Longtown. There was another small station between Harker and Longtown, called Lyneside, a rarely photographed place, it seems. Ivatt Class 2 2-6-2T No 41264, built at Crewe in 1950, remained in traffic until December 1966, one of the last eight to survive.** Derek Cross

Left: **On 2 August 1964 Class A1 Pacific No 60131 *Osprey* approaches Rockcliffe on the WCML, having travelled along the link from Longtown to the West Coast main line south of Gretna Junction with a train of empty stock. This line gives access, via a flyover built in 1963, to Kingmoor Yard. The train is recorded as an Edinburgh Craigentinny–Leeds working, perhaps connected with holiday traffic. This tended to be much more defined by area in the 1960s, with events such as Wakes weeks in England and the Glasgow Fair in Scotland.** Derek Cross

Left: **Class V2 2-6-2 No 60816 was one that the author's father had footplated from Dundee to Millerhill across both the Tay and the Forth bridges. It was, he said, an unforgettable experience. At the end of July 1963, No 60816 (built in 1937 at Darlington) is seen on a Millerhill–Kingmoor freight near Rockcliffe on the approach to Kingmoor New Yard, having travelled over the spur from Longtown to just south of Gretna to gain access.** Derek Cross

Left: **Ivatt Class 4 No 43040 arrives at the south end of Kingmoor Yard with a long train of hopper wagons in April 1964. This picture shows the topography and the relationships between the lines at this end of the new yard. Clearly some track has only recently been laid. Going across the top of the picture is the Waverley route, with Hawick to the left and Carlisle to the right. Underneath, beside the end of the train, is the West Coast main line, and on the right above the second wagon is the new headshunt constructed in 1962/3 to give access from the new yard to the northbound Waverley route. The new yard signalbox is visible on the left. This access is still open today, serving the Carlisle freight terminal about a mile and a half away along the former Waverley route.** Derek Cross

Right: **In April 1965, nearly-new Brush Type 4 diesel No D1649 accelerates away from Carlisle with a northbound oil train. The 'X' headcode denotes a special working, complete with barrier wagons. The destination is presumed to be Millerhill Yard in Edinburgh. No D1649 later became Class 47/4 No 47 535, equipped to supply electric train heating, and in 1982 was named** *University of Leicester*. Derek Cross

Right: **Close to Kingmoor, just north of Carlisle but on the Waverley route, Ivatt Class 2 2-6-0 No 46455 works tender-first on an early morning passenger train on 30 July 1965. The photographer recorded it as the regular Carlisle–Harker workers' train, though the luggage van on the rear might suggest that the train is for Langholm. With another of the class, No 46458, allocated to Carlisle Upperby, this locomotive was a regular on the Keswick branch.** Derek Cross

Right: **On 2 April 1966 Derek Cross set off for Shap with the author, then aged 11, only to find that a major snowfall had badly disrupted both the West Coast main line and the Settle–Carlisle line, his intended destinations. A trip to see the shed foreman at Kingmoor depot revealed that everything was running late, that the diesels had not coped with the snow, and that if the visitors stayed at Kingmoor there would be lots to see. We took up a position on the bridge that carried the Waverley route over the West Coast main line, thereby getting the best of both worlds. Here the 7.06am Edinburgh Waverley–Carlisle approaches its journey's end (due in at 10.07am) behind BRCW/Sulzer Type 2 diesel No D5316.** Derek Cross

Above: **Technically this is not a Waverley-route service but an inter-yard transfer from Kingmoor to Upperby, Durranhill or Currock, the other yards in Carlisle. The train is Target 40, and the locomotive is a very dirty Ivatt Class 4 2-6-0, No 43139. The picture was taken in April 1966 from the Waverley-route formation just before it passes over the West Coast main line. The train is heading south and west on the new single line that was built when Kingmoor Yard was constructed in the early 1960s. The large, modern concrete road bridge, at the south end of Kingmoor Yard and on the right of the photograph, is still there today.** Derek Cross

Below: **A snowy 2 April 1966 sees the first Ivatt Class 4 2-6-0, No 43000, built at Horwich in December 1947. The first three members of this class, Nos 43000-2, were the only true LMS locomotives, the other 159 being built under British Railways auspices. The locomotive is very clearly allocated to the local shed, Kingmoor (12A). The train is a Saturday-morning freight to Hawick, perhaps with goods to be dropped off along the 45-mile route.** Derek Cross

Top: This bridge carried the Waverley route over the West Coast main line, just north of Carlisle. Immediately to its left is Kingmoor steam shed on the up side of the WCML, and to the right (on the down side) is Kingmoor new yard. The train is a long mixed freight on the Waverley route heading away from Carlisle towards Longtown. The locomotive is local Ivatt Class 4 2-6-0 No 43139. Built at Doncaster in 1951, it was withdrawn in September 1967. Derek Cross

Above: This picture was taken at Canal Bank in Carlisle in July 1964 and shows an excursion from Carlisle to Silloth, a port on the West Cumberland coast 22 miles from Carlisle. This branch had been built by the North British Railway (NBR). The locomotives are GNSR 4-4-0 No 49 *Gordon Highlander* (later BR Class D40 No 62277), built in 1920, and Caledonian Railway single No 123, built in 1886 in Glasgow. Both are now preserved in Glasgow. Peter Brock

Top: **The southbound 'Waverley' stands in the platform at Carlisle Citadel station on 5 August 1967. The train has arrived over the Waverley route behind green 'Peak' No D16 and will go forward over the Settle & Carlisle line to Leeds behind the same locomotive. Steam on BR had just about a year left, but some of the habits of the steam age had transferred to diesels, as attested by the '55A' (Leeds Holbeck) shed plate, painted yellow.**
Derek Cross

Above: **One Saturday at the south end of Carlisle Citadel in August 1967, a Dundee–Blackpool train has just arrived, via the Waverley route, behind Edinburgh Haymarket English Electric Type 4 No D358. The diesel will be detached here and replaced by LMS Class 5 4-6-0 No 44802, which is waiting in the centre road for the passenger train to arrive. A very full tender of coal indicates that it has just come from Kingmoor shed and is well prepared for the climb to Shap and on to Blackpool via Preston. Such was the volume of traffic on a summer Saturday that the aim was to get the locomotives changed and able to depart as soon as possible.**
Derek Cross

Above: Two named locomotives are seen here at the north end of Carlisle station in August 1950; they are Class B1 4-6-0 No 61221 *Sir Alexander Erskine-Hill* and 'Coronation' Pacific No 46232 *Duchess of Montrose*. The 'B1' is setting off briskly with a Carlisle–Edinburgh train via the Waverley route. On the other side of Carlisle No 4 signalbox, the 'Duchess' waits to replace the locomotive on an incoming train from the south and take its train on to Glasgow Central via Beattock. Derek Cross

Below: Setting off from a then fully roofed Carlisle station on 8 August 1950 is the 'Thames-Forth' from Edinburgh to London St Pancras via the Waverley route and the Settle & Carlisle line. The train engine is Class 5 4-6-0 No 44716, being piloted by unrebuilt 'Patriot' 4-6-0 No 45516 *The Bedfordshire and Hertfordshire Regiment*. Both locomotives have the plain 'BRITISH RAILWAYS' inscription on their tenders. It seems likely that the locomotive that brought the train from Waverley has been replaced by this somewhat unusual combination. Derek Cross

Above: **Class V2 2-6-2 No 60964, as yet unnamed, passes Carlisle No 4 signalbox in early July 1951 with the up 'Thames–Forth' from Edinburgh Waverley to London St Pancras, comprising a uniform rake of Mk 1 carriages in carmine and cream (also known as 'blood and custard'), complete with destination boards. No 60964 was named *The Durham Light Infantry* in 1958, and remained in traffic until 1964.** Derek Cross

Below: **This two-coach local, forming the 4.13pm Carlisle–Riccarton Junction, passes the Caledonian yard north of Carlisle Citadel station some time in 1957. Pressed into service that day is Holmes-designed Class J36 0-6-0 No 65316, essentially a freight locomotive and a member of the largest class (168 in all) on the North British Railway. No 65316 was built at Cowlairs Works in Glasgow in April 1899, and remained in service until December 1962.** Peter Brock

Top: **The 'Metrovick' Type 2 Co-Bo diesels were part of the Carlisle freight scene in the late 1950s and 1960s, first in pairs with the 'Condor' service from London to Glasgow and later on as the regular power on trains to and from Workington and West Cumberland. Here, on the line to Workington with Carlisle in the background, is a pair of them, Nos D5715 and D5702. They were allocated Class 28 but had all been condemned before renumbering had taken place. Both these locomotives were new in 1958/9, and they were both withdrawn in 1968. After the 'Condor' ceased, 'Co-Bo's were rare in Scotland; eight examples were, however, moved to Shettleston, near Glasgow, for scrap in 1968. They are not thought to have been tried on the Waverley** route in any serious way. One of the class, No D5705, survives on the East Lancashire Railway at Bury, where it is slowly being restored to serviceable condition.
Peter Brock

Above: **This spring 1961 picture shows Class A3 Pacific No 60096 *Papyrus* crossing the North British bridge over the River Eden on the outskirts of Carlisle with the 10.5am from Edinburgh Waverley to London St Pancras, a not uncommon working for an 'A3' Pacific in 1961. Later that year No 60096 would be fitted with the German-style smoke-deflectors, retained these until withdrawal in July 1964.** Peter Brock

Left: **On 9 July 1961 a pair of Class B1 4-6-0s, No 61242 *Alexander Reith Gray* leading No 61290 behind, on an RCTS special from Leeds to Hawick/Tweedmouth and back, negotiate the Carlisle goods lines, passing Bog Junction signalbox (right) and the famous factory of Carlisle crane makers Cowans Sheldon (left). The same train, passing Whitrope, is illustrated elsewhere in this book. The leading locomotive is obviously allocated to Kittybrewster shed (61A) and is thus a very long way from its home shed.** Peter Brock

Below left: **This picture was taken in September 1961 from the footplate of 'Jubilee' 4-6-0 No 45574 *India* while held at signals at Willowholme Junction, just north of Carlisle. Visible is Class A3 Pacific No 60068 *Sir Visto* coming off the Waverley route and into Citadel station with an up express.** Peter Brock

Above right: **Filthy Gateshead-based Class A4 Pacific No 60002 *Sir Murrough Wilson* approaching St Nicholas Bridge, on the outskirts of Carlisle, in 1962. The train is the up 'Waverley' from Edinburgh to St Pancras, with the 'A4' either substituting for the more regular 'Peak' diesel or having been 'borrowed' for the duty.** Peter Brock

Right: **Class A3 Pacific No 60100 *Spearmint* accelerates away from Carlisle with a northbound Waverley-route express to Edinburgh in 1962. The photographer noted that the Gresley Pacific was substituting for a failed diesel, and had had to be prepared quickly at Carlisle Canal shed for this express passenger train. *Spearmint* was fitted with German-style smoke-deflectors in August 1961. With Nos 60041 and 60052, it was one of the last three 'A3s' to remain in traffic. All worked regularly over the Waverley route. The class were all out of service by January 1966, the one survivor being probably the most famous of them all, No 4472 *Flying Scotsman*, which is at present being rebuilt at the National Railway Museum in York.** Peter Brock

Above: **A northbound stopping train in one of the bay platforms at the north end of Carlisle Citadel on 18 August 1962. On the left is the Waverley-route train to Hawick from Platform 8, behind BRCW/Sulzer Type 2 No D5301, which departed at 6.13pm. On the right is rebuilt 'Royal Scot' 4-6-0 No 46107 *Argyll and Sutherland Highlander*, on the 6.10pm train from Platform 7 to Glasgow via Dumfries and Kilmarnock. Today these platforms are still used by trains to Glasgow via the Nith Valley and to Girvan and Stranraer with connections at Carlisle to and from 'the South', as English destinations tend to be known in Scotland.** Derek Cross

Left: **Local workers' trains survived even into the 1960s. They were used to take large numbers of workers from a station to a plant or factory, be they railway workshops, private factories or, as in this case, a military site. Pictured here in April 1963, crossing the Waverley-route bridge over the River Eden in Carlisle, Ivatt Class 4 2-6-0 No 43139 heads the 8.10am workers' train to Parkhouse Halt, 3 miles away.** Peter Brock

Above: **Station pilots in those days could be seen at a number of places, including Edinburgh Waverley and Hawick. On 14 April 1965, Ivatt Class 2 2-6-2T No 41217 is performing the same duty at Carlisle Citadel station. It is pictured in a siding on the east side, resting between duties. Behind the locomotive is what appears to be a wooden horsebox, perhaps no longer in regular use by this time. No 41217 was built at Crewe in September 1948, and remained in traffic until December 1966, making it another locomotive with a working life of less than 20 years.** Derek Cross

Below: **BRCW/Sulzer Type 2 diesel No D5302, departs from Platform 7 at Carlisle Citadel station on a wet 14 April 1965. The train is a stopping service from Carlisle to Edinburgh Waverley, with a typical Waverley-route consist of vans and passenger carriages. The main southbound Platform 4 at Carlisle is adjacent at the north end to bay Platform 7, from which this service departs. No D5302, new to Hornsey in North London in October 1958, remains in existence today on the Strathspey Railway at Boat of Garten, albeit unrestored.** Derek Cross

Above: **Both the north and south ends of Carlisle station in the 1960s often allowed photographers to get three or even four locomotives lined up together for the master shot. At the north end of the station on 14 April 1965 the author's father has managed to capture three different classes all in a line. On the left in the platform is Class B1 4-6-0 No 61330, waiting for an inward Waverley-route train to take back out; Class 3F 'Jinty' 0-6-0 No 47326 is the station pilot on this wet April day, while Class 5 4-6-0 No 45097 is accelerating away with a train from Morecambe to Glasgow Central. By the end of 1966, all three locomotives had been withdrawn.** Derek Cross

Left: **In August 1965, a Waverley-route stopping train, behind BRCW/Sulzer Type 2 No D5306, is seen in the bay platform at Carlisle Citadel while a Blackpool–Glasgow train, behind Class 5 4-6-0 No 45293, restarts on its way to the border at Gretna and on via Beattock to Glasgow Central. Again, judging by the coal heaped up in the tender, the steam locomotive has just taken over the train. No 45293 was built by Armstrong-Whitworth in 1936, and is at present being restored at the Colne Valley Railway in Essex.** Derek Cross

Above: **Summer Saturdays brought many holiday trains to Carlisle, and several of them changed locomotives in Citadel station. This photograph, taken on 14 August 1965, shows a Dundee–Blackpool train, which has just arrived over the Waverley route behind a very clean Class V2 2-6-2, No 60955, which gave way to local Class 5 4-6-0 No 44903 for the onward journey to Blackpool.** Derek Cross

Right: **This other named train between St Pancras to Scotland was the 'Thames–Clyde Express'. As the driver walks away from the locomotive, 'Peak' diesel No D99, the second man is already topping up the train heating boiler from the steam locomotive water column at the end of the main northbound platform at Carlisle Citadel. Also of note are the mail and parcels being loaded into the train, destined for Dumfries, Kilmarnock and Glasgow. It looks as though No D99 had not yet been named *Third Carabinier*, which dates this picture as before December 1965.** British Railways London Midland Region

Above: **The goods lines around Carlisle were extensive and vital to coping with the sheer volume of freight traffic associated with the border city; it was also important to try to keep freight out of Citadel station. Here, near Bog Junction and close to the end of steam at Carlisle in 1967, BR Pacific No 70003 (the former** *John Bunyan* **and Derek Cross's favourite 'Britannia') sets off southwards with a freight that had originated at Kingmoor Yard.** Peter Brock

Top right: **Builder's plate No 9155 of March 1899 reveals that this is Holmes Class J36 0-6-0 No 65312, pictured out of service during maintenance at Carlisle Canal shed in 1961. Passed cleaner Robert Taylor, a friend of the photographer, is seen in a most unusual position — purely for the sake of the photograph, one hopes. Just imagine how dirty he was after this 'expedition' down the chimney. It also gives some scale to the size of the steam locomotive, albeit in this case a relatively small Class J36!** Peter Brock

Top far right: **When the 1960s arrived and diesels began to replace steam, locomotives not previously seen in certain parts of the country began to appear. They included Gresley's famous Class A4 Pacifics, which, late in their working lives, not only worked the Glasgow–Aberdeen three-hour expresses but were also seen from time to time on the Waverley route. In this 1960 picture Peter Brock is sitting in the cab of No 60001** *Sir Ronald Matthews* **within the confines of Carlisle Canal shed, perhaps imagining** what it would have been like to descend from Essendine at 100mph! Peter Brock collection

Right: **Note the haircuts, the clothes, the notebook and the enthusiasm in these early 1960s trainspotters! Pictured at Carlisle Canal in about 1961, these two boys are clearly animated by 'Crab' 2-6-0 No 42836. Quite why is uncertain, as the locomotive had been a Kingmoor engine for many years. Such excitement, the pointing, and perhaps jumping up and down, normally only took place when a 'cop' had been made — in plain English, when a locomotive that had not been seen before was spotted. Had the complete LMS works plate been visible, it would have been found to read 'No 2836', built in Horwich in July 1930. The locomotive was withdrawn in December 1962.** Peter Brock

Far right: **The same two boys pictured with 'Crab' 2-6-0 No 42836 are seen again here, this time with their pedal car. Clearly the pair of BRCW/Sulzer Type 2 diesels and BR/Sulzer No D5096, new to Gateshead depot in April 1960, are of only passing interest to the driver of the pedal car.** Peter Brock

Far left: **Three young men of Canal shed, Messrs Eccles, Taylor and Thompson, pose alongside visiting Gresley Class A4 Pacific No 60004** *William Whitelaw* **in 1962.** Peter Brock

Far right: **Driver Tommy Gray at the end of his shift on the footplate in Citadel station, showing once again that driving steam locomotives was a pretty dirty job. Tommy Gray held the record for the number of steam runs between Carlisle and London on the famous freight train, the 'Condor', scheduled for 'Metrovick' Type 2 ('D57xx') diesels in pairs. These early diesels were very unreliable and steam often had to substitute. Tommy always had to keep time, on the quicker diesel timings, and his regular fireman, Frankie Phillips, was still having back pains as a result, 30 years later!** Peter Brock

Below left: **Numerically the first BR Class A4 Pacific, No 60001** *Sir Ronald Matthews* **is in a hurry to leave Canal shed to take over the down 'Waverley' at Citadel station in May 1962. This Gateshead-allocated 'A4' became a regular visitor to Carlisle Canal after the 'Deltics' had usurped the 'A4s' from top-link work on the East Coast main line. No 60001 had carried the name** *Garganey*

before 1948, and despite its number it was actually the fifth-last 'A4' to be built, in April 1938. It is reported that numbers were allocated out of sequence to ensure that the early numbers were given to locomotives named after LNER directors. Peter Brock

Below: **Peter Brock more or less had the run of Carlisle Canal, and was able to take this picture in summer 1962. It shows nine locomotives, representing seven classes, steam and diesel, such was the variety of motive power in the last years of the Waverley route. Identifiable are BRCW/Sulzer Type 2 No D5310 (nowadays preserved in Wales), Fairburn Class 4 2-6-4T No 42098 (built at Brighton and at one time allocated to Tunbridge Wells shed), 'Crab' 2-6-0 No 42720, Class V2 2-6-2 No 60816 and Class A3 Pacific No 60087** Blenheim. Peter Brock

126

Far left: **Class B1 4-6-0 No 61222, a Waverley-route regular, is seen here at Carlisle in April 1963, in the capable hands of driver Tommy McBride. Folklore has it that Tommy was very fond of fresh mushrooms, and on the sleepy NBR Silloth branch would often stop his train, pick a couple of pounds of mushrooms from the Burgh Marsh, get back on to the footplate and carry on. Whether the trains concerned were freight or passenger is not known.** Peter Brock

Left: **The chief Carlisle Canal firedropper, Dickie Reed, hangs on to the footplate of Ivatt Class 4 2-6-0 No 43040 and hitches a ride to the disposal pit. The young fireman seems more interested in Peter Brock, the photographer. Peter records that right at the end of Dickie's career, those 'new' locomotives (built in July 1949 at Horwich) that eventually got to Carlisle Canal had rocking grates, which made dropping their fires much easier.** Peter Brock

Below left: **Named freight locomotives were not common, but the Class J36 0-6-0s were named after events and personalities from World War 1. This one is No 65216 *Byng*, which was named after Julian Hedworth George Byng, famous for commanding the victory at Vimy Ridge in 1917 and later Governor General of Canada. Here the locomotive is at rest on its home shed, Carlisle Canal, complete with '68E' shed plate. Built as long ago as January 1890 at Cowlairs for the NBR, it was one of a class of 168 and was scrapped in 1962 after 72 years in traffic.** Neville Stead

Above right: **In purely photographic terms, locomotive sheds offer good artistic opportunities, owing to the contrasts of light and dark, as in this fine study of a group of drivers and firemen framed by the entrance to Carlisle Canal shed in 1960. The Class A2 Pacific in the distance is thought to be No 60519 *Honeyway*.** Peter Brock

Right: **Passed fireman Walter Tickler completes a brake test on Class A1 Pacific No 60118 *Archibald Sturrock* at Carlisle station. Compared with the older Class A3s, the A1s had the advantage of an independent steam brake, which was safer than the vacuum brake when the steam pressure was low. No 60118 was built at Doncaster in 1948, and was withdrawn and scrapped in 1965 after only 17 years in traffic.** Peter Brock

Saturday, 15 June 1963 was the last working day at Carlisle Canal shed (or MPD as it was perhaps better known in those days). All the men on duty on that shift — drivers, firemen and fitters — were assembled by the photographer to have their photograph taken on Stanier Class 4MT 2-6-4T No 42634, which prior to its transfer to Carlisle had been a resident of Accrington shed (24A). Once the photograph had been taken the 20 men dispersed, and fireman Peter Brock and his driver set off for Langholm with No 42634 on the 5.18pm train from Citadel station. Peter Brock